PRAEGER LIBRARY OF U.S. GOVERNMENT DEPARTMENTS
AND AGENCIES

The Bureau of the Census

The Bureau of the Census

A. Ross Eckler

PRAEGER PUBLISHERS
New York · Washington · London

PRAEGER PUBLISHERS
111 Fourth Avenue, New York, N.Y. 10003, U.S.A.
5, Cromwell Place, London SW7 2JL, England

Published in the United States of America in 1972
by Praeger Publishers, Inc.

© 1972 by Praeger Publishers, Inc.

Library of Congress Catalog Card Number: 73–168337

This book is No. 33 in the series
Praeger Library of U.S. Government Departments and Agencies

Printed in the United States of America

To my wife,

Jennie Howe Eckler,

for her never failing support

and encouragement

Preface

It would be easy and probably reasonably correct, to assign to Ernest Griffith, a consulting editor for this series of volumes, a longtime personal friend, and a fellow alumnus of Hamilton College, primary responsibility for my undertaking to write this book. As a masterful practitioner of what has become known as the "soft sell," Dr. Griffith mentioned this Praeger series on several occasions before my retirement as Director of the Bureau of the Census in 1969. He may have felt that I had a special responsibility because Hamilton College is the only institution of higher learning that has had two of its graduates serve as Director (Simon N. D. North being the first).

Another reason for my undertaking this volume is the recurrent comment of friends and fellow professionals to the effect that someone ought to put the Census story in written form. Most of those expressing this view were probably influenced by developments at the Bureau during the past thirty years.

My first contact with Bureau of the Census staff took place in the early 1930's, in connection with research for a dissertation on the statistics of the electric light and power industry. The staff, with long experience in operations, proved well informed on the characteristics of the particular series they had been compiling but seemed to have little interest in the broader objectives of their work. Periodic contacts with the Census staff made a few years later, during my service with the Work Projects Administration, did not alter my first impressions.

Like many who were appointed to temporary positions to work on the 1940 census, I was chiefly interested in getting firsthand experience in this unique type of statistical operation. A number of my colleagues had come to the Bureau after a period of service in one of the emergency agencies created to deal with the Great Depression. A large proportion of the newcomers consisted of recent college graduates, who were glad to accept temporary clerical posts as a means of getting some kind of work in a period of large-scale unemployment. A number of them moved to much more important roles in later years.

The dynamic developments in the Bureau of the Census in the years that followed can be traced to a number of factors. First, the leadership of Director J. C. Capt—a businessman with no previous experience in statistics—was notable for the support he gave to good management and the achievement of high standards of quality. Second, the demand for the Bureau's product increased rapidly because of the marked growth in the use of statistics for decision-making, both in government and in private industry. Third, there was dramatic progress in the application of mathematical principles in statistical work of all kinds, reflected in great advances in sampling, response research, evaluation, and over-all survey design and systems analysis. Fourth, there was a veritable revolution in all phases of statistical operation, based largely, but by no means completely, on the application of electronic computers to the task of data processing.

Anyone who looks for a recurring theme in this book will probably find it in the frequent reference to the role of the Census Bureau in the total federal statistical system. As noted in the first chapter, statistical organization came up for discussion as early as the 1840's. The issue has been a durable and dependable one and has led to a series of fairly consistent recommendations in the reports of a number of commissions and expert groups. Although the latest commission on statistics gave only limited consideration to organization, the Office of Budget and Management issued a directive in the summer of 1971, which led to reorganization in two departments by the end of the year.

I fully recognize that my account of these and other developments may suffer seriously from lack of objectivity because of my thirty years of service with the Bureau, but I have sought to avoid giving the reader the impression that I am assuming credit for the advances described. It is true that for twenty exciting years I served either as deputy director or as Director, but I would emphasize that the operation was at all times a team effort, the success of which was made possible by the dedication, drive, and enthusiasm of a great many people. The names of a number of them appear in this book, but there are many more who likewise deserve mention in any account of the Bureau's work. Those responsible for administering a large organization can perhaps render the greatest service by helping to maintain an environment favorable to research, innovation, and promotion of the public interest generally.

I am deeply grateful to many individuals for exceptional efforts in helping me to assemble the information presented in this book and in calling my attention to errors and omissions. They must receive credit for many significant improvements, but they have no responsibility for any of the errors that remain.

My successor as Director, George Hay Brown, has been most gracious in giving support and encouragement to my undertaking.

I am particularly indebted to a number of senior officials for major help in the broad planning of the volume, in shaping my points of view on many issues, and in reviewing and criticizing the drafts of one or more of the chapters. In particular, Conrad Taeuber and Joseph Daly (now retired) have each been helpful on significant fractions of the book. Walter Ryan and William Merkin have also responded generously with valuable information in certain areas.

The services of Edwin Goldfield, William Stiver, Merle Bollard, Paul Taff, Walter Beller, Matthew Erickson, Samuel Maslak, Dorothy Kaufman and her excellent library staff, and the Public Information Office of the Bureau have been indispensable in enabling me to assemble the charts, tables, photographs, and reference materials in the text and in the appendixes.

Edward Swan, the only member of the Bureau staff to have read the entire manuscript, has called my attention to several ambiguous and misleading statements and, in addition, has made many important editorial comments. On the basis of suggestions from Mr. Swan, several chapters were referred for comment and correction to a number of Bureau specialists, including Anthony Berlinsky, Phyllis Carter, Joseph Freeman, Benjamin Gura, Melvin Hendry, Thomas Jabine, Daniel Levine, Lawrence Marzetti, Morton Meyer, and Dino Villa.

Important contributions to the book have been made by a number of former employees of the Bureau. Calvert L. Dedrick reviewed the initial drafts of a number of chapters and made many important suggestions, particularly in areas relating to early history, confidentiality provisions, and apportionment. Valuable comments on one or more chapters have been made by Harvey Kailin, Julius Shiskin, and Leon E. Truesdell. I wish to note especially the valuable assistance rendered by Robert Drury, both when he was deputy director and after his premature retirement early in 1971.

I am most grateful for the services of Ann McBride, who has cheerfully devoted much of her spare time during her evenings and weekends to typing the original draft and successive revisions of this work.

Finally, I would acknowledge my considerable debt to the highly capable editors responsible for this series of volumes. The comments and criticism of Hugh Elsbree, Lois O'Neill, Malinda Elliott, and Fred Howard have been most perceptive and helpful.

A. ROSS ECKLER

Washington, D.C.
March, 1972

Contents

LIST OF TABLES AND CHARTS

Tables

Charts

A section of photographs follows page 80.

The Bureau of the Census

I

The First Twelve Censuses 1790-1900

I often say that when you can measure what you are speaking about and express it in numbers you know something about it; but, when you cannot measure it, when you cannot express it in numbers, your knowledge is of a meagre and unsatisfactory kind: it may be the beginning of knowledge, but you have scarcely, in your thoughts, advanced to the stage of science whatever the matter may be.—LORD KELVIN

The above words were part of a lecture delivered by Lord Kelvin to an audience of engineers in 1883. They would have been just as fitting if they had been addressed to an audience of statisticians.

In all census taking, the central importance of measurement has been evident from the earliest known efforts down to the present. The purposes of the censuses have been broadened, and the methods used for census taking have changed radically, but the value of the operation itself was as well known to the rulers of ancient kingdoms as to the government officials and social scientists of our own times.

Over four thousand years ago, surveys of the extent, value, and ownership of land were taken in order to carry out taxation in ancient Babylon, China, and Egypt. Records were compiled to determine the military strength of the Hebrews at the time of the Exodus, about 1500 B.C., and again by King David, five hundred years later. Rome instituted district censuses for taxation and military purposes about 550 B.C., and in 5 B.C. Julius Caesar extended them to include the entire Roman Empire. Extant Peruvian records show undated early Inca counts for military purposes. The first census of Spain's American possessions was taken in A.D. 1577, under the orders of King Philip II.

Although a good deal of detailed research remains to be done on the origins of census taking, the principal purposes of the early censuses are well known. They provided information on one or both of the following subjects: (1) the manpower available for military use and (2) the number of people and the extent of their possessions as a basis for levying taxes. In view of the purposes for which censuses were taken in early times and the fragmentary evidence of the results, it appears unlikely that any of the returns made by citizens were subject to confidential treatment. There is some indication, however, that citizens were required to make returns and in some cases even to testify by oath to the correctness of the information supplied.

EARLY AMERICAN CENSUSES

Enough censuses were taken in the colonial period and the years of the Confederation in North America to provide a good deal of experience with such operations, even though the results were of uneven quality. Before the Revolution, inquiries were made primarily because of the interest of the British Board of Trade; those made during and after the Revolution were largely to evaluate sharing of the financial burden of the war. Thirty-eight different censuses, covering ten geographical areas, were taken before 1790, but there were a few areas for which the 1790 enumeration was to be the first. A historic precedent had been set for the use of census statistics by the Constitutional Convention of 1787. Article 1, Section 2, of the Constitution stated:

Representatives and direct taxes shall be apportioned among the several States which may be included within this Union, according to their respective numbers, which shall be determined by adding to the number of free persons, including those bound to service for a term of years, and excluding Indians not taxed, three-fifths of all other persons. The actual enumeration shall be made within three years after the first meeting of the Congress of the United States, and within every subsequent term of ten years, in such manner as they shall by law direct.

The significance of this provision of the American Constitution was recognized by the French statistician Moreau de Jonnes, who declared that the United States presented a phenomenon without parallel in history, "that of a people who instituted the statistics of their country on the very day when they founded their government, and who regulated by the same instrument the census of inhabitants, their civil and political rights, and the destinies of the nation."

Thanks to the efforts of James Madison, even the first national census was not restricted to the minimum requirement stated in the Constitution. Madison saw that knowledge regarding the numbers of persons engaged in various arts and professions is useful in providing for the diverse interests of the country. He also recognized the military and industrial needs for census information and initiated separate counts of white males over sixteen and under sixteen. His proposals, which were not pertinent to the apportionment of representatives, were approved by the House but not by the Senate.

From the point of view of a student of governmental structure and functions, the early placing of census responsibility in the central government may have been an important factor in accounting for the relatively small role played by the states in influencing the scope and character of the decennial censuses. A number of states have taken their own censuses, notably in fields of population and manufacturing, but there has been relatively little interchange of ideas and suggestions between the federal government and the states in this area, even though officials with experience in state censuses have been utilized on a number of occasions in the national census. In some other countries—Canada and Australia, for instance—the states or provinces have been quite influential in census operations; in Germany, the states (*Länder*) have been able to add their own questions to the forms developed for the country as a whole.

The first twelve U.S. decennial censuses were taken by temporary organizations created specifically to carry out the provisions of the corresponding census act, the first of which was approved on March 1, 1790. Table I gives the supervising department and the official or officials responsible for each of the first twelve censuses from 1790 to 1900.

It is not at all surprising that, during the tenure of this long series of temporary census organizations, there should have been recurrent demands for a permanent census organization. Such demands must have been sparked by the recognition that it is highly inefficient to assemble and dismantle a complete statistical organization every ten years. It must also have become apparent that taking the census of a population provides a statistical experience that might be advantageously applied to other undertakings of a statistical nature. In the United States, as in many other countries, one of the first large-scale statistical activities was the taking of a census. This normally involved the creation of a sizable temporary field organization for collection of the information, as well as a large clerical staff to process the results. In the later years of

TABLE I

DEPARTMENT AND OFFICIALS RESPONSIBLE FOR THE FIRST
TWELVE U.S. CENSUSES, 1790–1900

Year	Department	Official and Title
1790	State	Thomas Jefferson, Secretary [a]
1800	State	John Marshall, Secretary
1810	State	Robert Smith, Secretary
1820	State	John Quincy Adams, Secretary
1830	State	Martin Van Buren, Secretary
1840	State	William A. Weaver, Superintending Clerk
1850	Interior	Joseph Camp Griffith Kennedy, Superintendent James Dunwoody Bronson DeBow, Superintendent
1860	Interior	Joseph Camp Griffith Kennedy, Superintendent
1870	Interior	Francis Amasa Walker, Superintendent
1880	Interior	Francis Amasa Walker, Superintendent Charles William Seaton, Superintendent
1890	Interior	Robert Percival Porter, Superintendent
1900	Interior	William Rush Merriam, Director

[a] Degree of responsibility of Secretary of State in 1790 is not clear.

the nineteenth century, there was also a need for specialized equipment, much of which was created primarily for use in the census. Finally, those who plan and supervise large organizations form a cadre experienced in the management of large-scale statistical undertakings. In the absence of a continuing organization, however, there was little opportunity for the transfer of this collective experience, since the field and office workers were separated from the rolls as soon as the work on a particular census had been completed.

There was some progress in the centralization of statistical work in other parts of the world prior to 1900. For example, in Germany centralization took place in 1872; the Central Statistics Bureau of Norway was established in 1875; the Central Statistical Office of the Kingdom of Hungary was set up in 1897; and the Central Bureau of Statistics in the Netherlands was created in 1899.

DEMANDS FOR A PERMANENT CENSUS ORGANIZATION

It is difficult to establish the date of the first recommendation for a permanent Bureau of the Census, but in Wright and Hunt's *History and Growth of the United States Census,* compiled some seventy years ago, reference is made to pressure for such a change after the census of 1840. A select committee of the House of Representatives concluded that the errors in this census formed a strong argument for establishment of a Bureau of Statistics.

From reports prepared by the House committee in 1844 and 1845, it seems reasonable to conclude that proposals were aimed not only at establishing a permanent organization for census work, but also at coordinating the statistical work of the federal government. A similar point of view was expressed in 1854 by Superintendent James D. B. DeBow:

> This office machinery exists in all European countries where statistics are the most reliable, but there has been none of it in the United States. Each census has taken care of itself. Every ten years some one at Washington will enter the hall of a department, appoint fifty or a hundred persons under him, who, perhaps, have never compiled a table before, and are incapable of combining a column of figures correctly. Hundreds of thousands of pages of returns are placed in the hands of such persons to be digested. If any are qualified, it is no merit of the system. . . . The establishment of a regular statistical office is, therefore, suggested, as a matter of economy, and essential to the proper execution of the census.

In each year from 1860 to 1865, the Secretary of Interior, in his annual report, made a statement regarding the need for a statistical bureau. The following quotation from his 1861 report is typical: "All enlightened foreign governments and several of the States sustain statistical bureaus, while the United States . . . have yet to institute such an agency." Obviously, if any of the recommendations in the 1840's and

1860's had been followed, the United States would have kept pace with developments in Europe.

It is possible that, during the Civil War and the Reconstruction period, other problems ruled out consideration of extensive changes in our statistical organization. At any rate, not until the 1890's was there a strong renewal of earlier drives for a permanent Bureau of the Census that could also serve as a central statistical bureau. The National Board of Trade in 1890 adopted resolutions for a committee to study the feasibility of a permanent statistical and enumerating staff and of a way to avoid concentrating inquiries in a single year. There followed a series of discussions in the Congress and consideration of proposals prepared by the Superintendent of the Census and submitted by the Secretary of the Interior. In the absence of definitive action on these proposals, the Congress passed a joint resolution asking the Commissioner of Labor to prepare for the Congress as soon as possible a plan for a permanent census service.

The case for a permanent Bureau was considerably strengthened by dissatisfaction with the 1890 census results and the time required to publish them. Two major professional associations, the American Economic Association and the American Statistical Association, presented a memorial to the Congress asking for consideration of plans for the 1900 census and the desirability of a permanent census office. Hearings on the proposed legislation took place in both houses of Congress in 1897, but, in the absence of any conclusion in either house, the whole matter was held over until the next Congress.

The culmination of all of the recommendations and efforts over many years toward the establishment of a permanent census organization was the adoption of the Permanent Census Act in March, 1902.* Under this Act, Census became a per-

---

* A letter that Dr. Walter F. Willcox, then ninety-nine years old, wrote to Morris Hansen on August 6, 1959, includes an entertaining explanation of the reason for a permanent bureau: "Director William R. Merriam handled Congress very cleverly; got a stunning group of girls on his staff,

manent rather than a temporary office and was given a rather diverse program of censuses and surveys to keep it busy between the decennial population censuses. For example, the 1902 law called for a mid-decade census of manufactures, for the annual compilation of vital statistics, and for compilations of data on the defective, dependent, and delinquent classes, on crime and related judicial matters, on urban social conditions, on religious bodies, and on public finance (indebtedness, valuation, taxation, and expenditures).

The 1902 Act was plainly designed to provide for a permanent office rather than to alter the role of the temporary office. Little or no broadening of the Director's role was apparent in the provision that he was to direct the taking of the census and "to perform such other duties as may be imposed upon him by law." Perhaps the most significant new feature was the provision for spreading the work by putting some of the reports on an annual or quinquennial basis, but on the whole the principal features of the Act had already been a part of the census program for several decades.

THE 110-YEAR RECORD

On the whole, it is surprising that the first twelve censuses were as successful as they were, considering some of the handicaps under which they were carried out. One matter of interest, in the light of the recent controversy over census inquiries, is the fact that despite the obligation of citizens to furnish information, there was no legislative provision until 1880 restricting the use of the individual information given by respondents. Currently, census taking is kept free of any connection with law enforcement agencies, but through 1870

nearly all of them, no doubt, wanted to remain in Washington, and in the Census Office (at least until they got married). These girls, I was told brought so much pressure on Congress that in 1902, or thereabouts, the office was made permanent, not for any scientific reason, but to keep the staff from being disbanded."

the enumeration of all censuses was carried out by assistants to the marshals, who executed the orders of the federal courts in each judicial district. Regardless of any administrative assurance about the treatment of the records, the use of these assistants for collection must have had an inhibiting influence upon some respondents.

The greatest handicap of all, however, was the necessity to create a strictly temporary structure for carrying out each of the successive censuses. Remedial action was long delayed, despite sixty years of strong recommendations to the contrary from the Congress, from the executive branch, and from outside the government, and despite innovations in a number of countries at a similar stage of economic development. In retrospect, it seems clear that the delay helped limit the role to be played by the new permanent office in the twentieth century.

II

The Bureau of the Census and the Government Statistical System

Because the Bureau of the Census possessed the skills and equipment necessary for taking a national population inventory, it became a prime candidate for other statistical tasks once it had been established as a permanent office. The provisions of the 1902 Act did, to be sure, provide for some distribution of census tasks over a ten-year period, but the decennial population census was a much larger task than any of the Bureau's other undertakings, and there continued to be sharp fluctuations in the size of the organization. It was obvious that the assignment of additional tasks to the census agency would not only utilize the experience gained from the census but would also facilitate the retention of a nucleus organization to be available for planning the next census.

LEGISLATIVE CHANGES, 1929–48

For almost three decades after the creation of a permanent office for census work, there was no significant change in census legislation. In the twenty-year period beginning with 1929, however, a number of laws were enacted that strengthened the censuses and paved the way for a stronger program for the collection of current statistical information. The most important single statute was the Act providing for the 1930 census. The Act, approved June 18, 1929, recognized the growing complexity of choosing specific census inquiries within broad subject fields and left determination of such questions to the Director of the Census subject to the approval of the Secretary of Commerce. (Later, the determination was given directly to the Secretary of Commerce, who in turn delegated it to the Director.) By contrast, the Act for the 1920 census had specified about twenty items each for the population and the agriculture censuses. The 1929 Act also provided for a census of distribution—the first major addition in the area of economic statistical activities since 1840, when the agriculture and mining censuses were first undertaken. Another feature of the 1929 Act was the provision for an automatic reapportionment of congressional districts following each decennial census in the absence of any other action by Congress. The Act provided for the use of the apportionment method known as major fractions (the method used for apportionment in 1910), but the President was required to report the distribution of seats by two methods —major fractions and equal proportions.

The ten-year period 1939–48 was remarkable for three separate, significant pieces of legislation pertaining to the census. The first, enacted on August 11, 1939, provided for a census of housing, requiring for the first time comprehensive information on dwelling units. Business organizations had indicated strong interest in the scope of this legislation, with the result that the legislation covered "utilities and equipment"; this was more specific than the 1929 Act with its reference simply to population and agriculture. In practice, however, government interests have received primary emphasis, and utilities and equipment data have been collected only when needed for government purposes.

In 1941, the Congress adopted for the first time the method of equal proportions for allocation among the states of seats in the House of Representatives. It was discovered after the 1940 census that the equal proportions method and the major fractions method * gave different results. The adoption of the equal proportions approach avoided a shift of one seat from Michigan to Arkansas that otherwise would have taken place.

The third piece of legislation in this period was Public Law 671, approved June 19, 1948, which revised certain parts of the basic statutes. The most important features of the 1948 Act were the revision of the time schedule for the economic censuses and the provision of a solid legislative base for the program of current statistics. It provided that the frequency of the census of manufactures be reduced from once in two years to once in five years and that the frequency of the censuses of business and mineral industries be increased from once in ten years to once in five. All these censuses were to be taken concurrently in the years ending in 3 and 8. The list of subjects to be included at five-year intervals included for the first time the field of transportation. The legislation also contained the phrase "and other businesses," which apparently was introduced to give the executive branch authority to add other categories at its discretion.

The 1948 Act gave strong support to current statistical surveys. Current reports could henceforth be requested from business concerns on a mandatory basis, provided: (1) the inquiries were similar to those included in authorized complete censuses; (2) adequate advance public notice of intent to conduct the survey was given; (3) a determination had been made that "the information called for is needed to aid or permit the efficient performance of essential governmental functions or services; or has significant application to the needs

* These are two of the methods which have been used for determining the number of representatives for each state. The reader wishing detail on methods and history is referred to Laurence F. Schmeckebier, *Congressional Apportionment* (Washington: Brookings Institution, 1941).

of the public, business, or industry and is not publicly available"; and (4) the survey was not carried out more than once a year.

THE FIRST THREE DECADES:
PRESSURES FOR CENTRALIZATION

It would have seemed fairly safe in 1902 to predict that the United States, like many European countries, would establish a central bureau of statistics. Such a development was facilitated by a provision of the 1903 law that transferred the Bureau of the Census to the new Department of Commerce and Labor. In the Organic Act for the new Department, the Secretary was given authority to reorganize the statistical work of his Department and to consolidate where necessary. In another section of the Act, the President was authorized to transfer to the Department of Commerce and Labor, from any other department (except Agriculture), the whole or part of any office, bureau, or division engaged in statistical work. (The exclusion of Agriculture seems to have been based more on political than statistical considerations.)

The hearings held by the Secretary of Commerce and Labor, as authorized by the Organic Act, demonstrated that centralization of statistics, if it requires reassignment of functions, will never be achieved by the democratic process. Centralization is unlikely except when ordered by a high-level official, fully convinced of the correctness of his point of view and willing to disregard strenuous representations about impairment of statistics, loss of control, and the lack of regard for administrative needs brought about by such transfers. Secretary Oscar Straus was probably encouraged to make such transfers by Director of the Census Simon N. D. North, since North saw clearly potential gains from a consolidation of statistical functions, but North had only limited influence with the Secretary, and their period of contact was marred by bitter controversy over the jurisdictional rights of the Bureau and the Department. The controversy centered around the authority to select and appoint temporary Bureau personnel, the name of the Bureau, the choice of a seal, centralization of the disbursing function, making census records available to the other agencies of the Department, and the failure of the Secretary to pass on to the Congress complaints from the Director. The controversy continued until the passage of the law for the 1910 census. Although this legislation apparently upheld some of the viewpoints of the Director, North resigned and was succeeded by E. Dana Durand, a Department statistician.

During this period of jurisdictional conflict, a committee appointed by the Secretary of Commerce and Labor held hearings to inquire into the statistical work of the Department. The committee, appointed in September, 1907, with the assistant secretary as chairman, included heads of bureaus of the Department. The two major proponents of consolidation at the hearings were Director North and a representative from the government of Canada, where the need for a central agency was clearly recognized. Without exception, Department witnesses, threatened with loss of some of their agencies' statistical functions, argued against any transfer, maintaining that no economy would result, since their statistical staffs were already fully and efficiently utilized. They predicted loss of efficiency if the statistical function was detached from their agencies' other programs, so it is not surprising that the Secretary of Commerce and Labor did not take advantage of his power to transfer and consolidate statistical work within his Department.

During the next decade, the consolidation of statistical work continued to be an issue. In the *American Statistical Association Quarterly* for June, 1914, William S. Rossiter proposed an Office of National Statistics, to include census, labor, agriculture, mining, and many other statistical functions. But the 1913 split of the Department into separate departments of Commerce and of Labor left the Secretary of Commerce with fewer possibilities for consolidation. Director Durand (1909–13) seemed more interested in statistical presentation than in consolidation. The need for additional statistical information, brought about by our entry into World War I, was met primarily by the creation of new emergency agencies. William A. Hathaway of the American Telephone and Telegraph Company reported in the *American Statistical Association Quarterly* for June, 1918, that the Bureau of the Census had confined its attention to peacetime investigations instead of engaging in war work. In the same article, Hathaway suggested that an Office of International Statistics be established to serve as an official clearinghouse for all statistical matters.

In the 1920's, two developments could have facilitated the movement toward centralization of the government's statistical work. One of these was the 1922 report of the Federal Bureau of Efficiency. This bureau had been set up originally in 1916; in 1919 it was specifically authorized to investigate duplication of statistical work in the government, as well as federal requirements for statistics and the methods used for meeting them. The major recommendation was for a large-scale transfer of statistical work to the Bureau of the Census, which would be renamed the Bureau of Federal Statistics. One important shift in the opposite direction was the proposed transfer of vital statistics (births, deaths) from the Bureau of the Census to the Public Health Service. The trend, however, was toward consolidation, as shown by the following quotation from the report of the Bureau of Efficiency:

> Centralization of the collection and dissemination of all non-administrative statistics within one bureau would result in the standardization and improvement of output; permit the consolidation of questionnaire schedules and inquiries, the more intensive use of machines, and the more economical employ-

ment of field agents; and provide one central office to which the public could apply for the great bulk of the statistical information collected by the Government. . . . The Bureau of the Census is the logical bureau in which to concentrate this work. It is the largest statistical unit of the Federal Government. Its sole function is the collection and dissemination of statistical information.

Another development in the 1920's that could have strengthened the Bureau's role in statistics was the appointment of Herbert Hoover as Secretary of Commerce. A member of the American Statistical Association and the International Statistical Institute, Hoover was keenly interested in the statistical work of his Department and acted vigorously to increase the number of statistical services rendered to business. In his 1924 report, the Bureau of the Census is referred to as "the central statistical agency of the Federal Government." However, William Mott Steuart, Director of the Bureau of the Census at that time, had an essentially conservative view of the Bureau's role and had little inclination to broaden its functions. He had worked on no less than five decennial censuses (1880–1920) and would have had little interest in reorganizing the agency along the lines recommended by the Federal Bureau of Efficiency.

CONTINUED DECENTRALIZATION

Developments beginning in 1933 represented a complete departure from those in earlier years and a movement away from the trends toward centralization in a number of other countries at a comparable stage of economic development. A number of factors had a bearing on this course of events. A Central Statistical Board was established by executive order on July 27, 1933, to coordinate the statistical services of the government and to facilitate the implementation of the National Industrial Recovery Act. This Board was composed of the secretaries of Agriculture, Commerce, and Labor, the Governor of the Federal Reserve Board, and members designated by the President and by the National Industrial Recovery Administration and the Committee on Government Statistics and Information Services. Additional members were elected by the Board itself. The relative weights of the agencies represented were quite uneven. The serious plight of American agriculture, the prestige of the Bureau of Agricultural Economics, and the influence of Secretary of Agriculture Henry A. Wallace greatly outweighed whatever influence the Department of Commerce might have had on the Central Statistical Board, and the problems of unemployment and low wages gave corresponding leverage to Secretary of Labor Frances Perkins and Commissioner of Labor Statistics Isador Lubin. Secretary of Commerce Daniel Roper had little chance to strengthen the statistical work of his Department at the expense of Agriculture and Labor, even if he had wanted to do so. At any rate, his case for such action was significantly weakened by the condition of the Census Bureau at this point in history.

After the completion of the 1930 census, the Bureau reduced its staff drastically to intercensal work levels, as required by the 1932 legislation, usually referred to as the Economy Act. This left the Bureau with only a skeleton staff, many of whom had joined the agency in 1902 and had little technical training in statistics. In 1933, the Bureau had only three Ph.D.'s and only one professional man under forty-five years of age. Secretary Roper and Director William Austin had neither the size nor type of staff necessary for participating in challenging New Deal activities. Nevertheless, the Bureau did direct some projects and assist new agencies with others. By 1938, its professional staff included a total of forty-two social scientists, out of the two thousand employed in the federal government as a whole.

At about the time of the establishment of the Central Statistical Board in 1933, the American Statistical Association, which had long taken an interest in greater centralization of federal statistics, organized (jointly with the Social Science Research Council) a Committee on Government Statistics and Information Services (COGSIS). From 1933 to 1937, the committee worked with the Central Statistical Board in carrying out a broad study of the entire federal statistical system. Its report, published in 1937, recommended a division of labor and decentralization of authority, based on the "focal agency" concept, under which departments or independent agencies became focal points for certain broad areas of statistical work. A coordinating agency was recommended as a means of dealing with the decentralized statistical system. These views reflected the strong preference of the Central Statistical Board itself, as set forth in its first annual report in 1934, for a focal statistical agency in each major field of information and for an over-all statistical coordinating agency that would collect no statistics on its own. The committee's recommendations for the Census Bureau considered the possibility that certain activities be transferred out of the Bureau —the collection of vital statistics and agricultural and mining statistics, for example.*

Subsequent administrative and legislative developments greatly strengthened the coordinating agency idea and reduced the prospect that the Bureau of the Census would become a central statistical bureau. The original Central Statistical Board was transferred to the Bureau of the Budget in 1939, thereby acquiring additional strength because of its connection with the vital budget-making process. Two later

* The author of this volume began his period of government service in 1935. His feeling at the time was that the Committee on Government Statistics and Information had some basis for their conclusions. The Census Bureau at that time was one of the least promising for anyone interested in a statistical career in the federal government. The number of professionals in the Bureau was still very small, and the general image of the organization was that of a slow-moving agency restricted to publishing statistics of the traditional sort in a number of fields prescribed by law.

acts, the Federal Reports Act of 1942 and the Budget and Accounting Procedures Act of 1950, provided support to the move to place the coordinating agency in the Bureau of the Budget. During the last thirty years, the coordinating function has been directed by a high official of the Bureau of the Budget—or of the Office of Management and Budget, as the Bureau of the Budget is now called.

The Hoover Commission of 1947 supported some modification of the existing system of statistical organization. In connection with the work of the Hoover Commission, the National Bureau of Economic Research was asked to undertake a survey of statistical agencies. The report of this survey, directed by Frederick C. Mills and Clarence D. Long, was published in 1949. The most important elements as far as the Bureau of the Census was concerned were recommendations 1 and 9. The first dealt with the principles of organization and administration and provided

> that the tasks of collecting, processing, and analyzing statistics be divided among . . . various agencies gathering statistics for use as instruments of management or as by-products of administrative or regulatory activities [as follows:] A single agency, qualified for economical mass enumeration and the efficient use of sampling procedures, serving the public and other agencies of government in repetitive and large-scale tasks of primary collection and tabulation. . . . A small number of agencies devoted to research and analysis in specialized fields and to limited primary collection calling for highly specialized knowledge of subject matter. . . . A small number of analytical agencies and advisory councils utilizing statistics collected and processed by other agencies.

The ninth recommendation, dealing with the division of functions among statistical agencies, included the following provision: "That the Bureau of the Census be designated the service agency of the Government for the primary collection and tabulation of statistics gathered on a repetitive basis, and for which highly specialized knowledge of subject matter is not required in the collection process."

The recommendations of the task force were somewhat modified in the final report by the Hoover Commission, which included the following statement regarding the role of the Census Bureau: "The Commission recommends that the diverse system of collecting and analyzing statistical data should be continued. It is suggested, however, that greater use should be made of the Census Bureau for the repetitive, large-scale tasks of primary collection and tabulation of statistical data."

Three years later, in the fall of 1952, a Temple University survey, designed to update the Hoover Commission Report and provide guidelines for the incoming Eisenhower Administration, supported the conclusions of the commission regarding greater centralization of statistical work. The section of the survey relating to the Commerce Department stated:

> The collection by the Federal Agencies of all statistics of a nature not highly technical or confidential should be transferred to the Census Bureau. . . . This is a recommendation of the Hoover Commission's Task Force on Statistical Agencies which has not been vigorously pursued. The Census Bureau is especially designed and operated to collect and process statistics of a "mass production" nature. To ensure use of its specialization and avoid duplication all statistical operations possible should be transferred to it.

THE BUREAU'S ROLE SINCE 1940

Several developments of major significance have taken place since 1940—some in line with, and some contrary to, the recommendations of the Hoover Commission and the Temple University survey. In 1942, responsibility for the Monthly Report on the Labor Force (now the Current Population Survey) was transferred to the Census Bureau by the

Bureau of the Budget. The Current Population Survey will be described in detail in Chapter V.

In 1946, the Division of Vital Statistics was transferred by the President's Reorganization Plan No. 2 to the Public Health Service, in order to keep it closer to the organization responsible for health grants to the states. This transfer has seemed inexplicable to statisticians of other countries where a single agency is usually responsible for both the numerator (births, deaths) and the denominator (population) of widely used vital ratios.

In 1959, two somewhat offsetting functional transfers were made. The Census Bureau was given responsibility for construction statistics, and certain activities were transferred to it from the Bureau of Labor Statistics and the Business and Defense Services Administration. At the same time, however, responsibility for planning and analyzing the section of the Current Population Survey pertaining to the labor force was transferred to the Bureau of Labor Statistics, although the Bureau of the Census retained responsibility for collecting and tabulating the data.

Such outright transfers of functions to the Bureau have been infrequent, whereas the amount of service work done for other agencies has increased sharply. The Bureau's growing involvement with other agencies can be attributed to several factors: (1) the development and retention of a highly skilled staff of professional statisticians and managerial personnel, (2) the facility for rapid collection and compilation of national sample surveys, (3) the development and adaptation of specialized data processing equipment, and (4) the Budget Bureau's efforts to implement the Hoover Commission's recommendations for greater centralization in the handling of mass data projects.

In the 1960's, the role of the Census Bureau in the federal structure again became a subject of discussion, largely because of the enormous increase in the use of electronic equip-

TABLE II. Growth of the Decennial Census, 1790–1970

Census Year	Total U.S. Population (millions)	Number of Enumerators [a]	Maximum Size of Office Force	Total Pages in Published Reports	Total Cost (thousands of dollars)	Cost Per Capita (cents)
1790	3.9	650 [b]	[c]	56	44	1.1
1800	5.3	900 [b]	[c]	74	66	1.2
1810	7.2	1,100 [b]	[c]	469	178	2.4
1820	9.6	1,188	[d]	288	208	2.1
1830	12.9	1,519	43	214	378	2.9
1840	17.1	2,167	28	1,465	833	4.8
1850	23.2	3,231	160	2,165	1,423	6.1
1860	31.4	4,417	184	3,189	1,969	6.3
1870	38.6	6,530	438	3,473	3,421	8.8
1880	50.2	31,382	1,495	21,458	5,790	11.4
1890	63.0	46,804	3,143	26,408	11,547	18.3
1900	76.2	52,871	3,447	10,925	11,854	15.5
1910	92.2	70,286	3,738 [e]	11,456	15,968	17.3
1920	106.0	87,234	6,301 [e]	14,550	25,117	23.7
1930	123.2	87,756	6,825 [e]	35,700	40,156	32.6
1940	132.2	123,069	9,987 [e]	58,400	67,527	51.1
1950	151.3	142,962	9,233	61,700	91,462	60.4
1960	179.3	159,321	2,960	103,000	127,934	71.4
1970	203.2	166,406	4,571	200,000	247,653 [f]	121.8

[a] Designated as assistants to the marshals, 1790–1870. [b] Estimated; records destroyed by fire. [c] None employed.
[d] Amount expended for clerk hire: $925.
[e] Includes all employees in years 1910–40. Most of the 700 to 900 in the permanent force were probably actually engaged in decennial operations at the peak period.
[f] At July, 1969, pay rates; covers some additional expenditures for tests of new procedures introduced in 1970.

ment and recognition of its potentialities for developing and storing statistics. The use of electronic equipment opens up the way to more effective utilization of the statistical information available in the government by greatly facilitating the matching of records and transfer of information. This possibility was an important reason for the establishment by the Bureau of the Budget of a special task force, referred to usually as the Kaysen Committee, to investigate the problem of storing and retrieving government statistics. One of the committee's recommendations involved the appointment of a director of a Federal Statistical System in the Executive Office of the President to coordinate the work of the Census Bureau and a proposed National Statistical Data Center.

In early 1969, the American Statistical Association, noting the lack of any recent, thorough study of federal statistics recommended a comprehensive review of the federal statistical program. As a result, President Richard M. Nixon in 1970 appointed a Commission on Federal Statistics under the chairmanship of Dr. W. Allen Wallis, a distinguished statistician, as well as chancellor, of the University of Rochester. The commission's report, issued late in 1971, recommended that the Census Bureau have major responsibility for two government-wide service functions: (1) central directories of industrial and other units and (2) an all-agency catalog of data held by the government.

Another development in 1971 was the issuance of a directive by the Office of Management and Budget to bring about some consolidation of statistical work in each of four departments (Agriculture; Commerce; Health, Education and Welfare; and Labor) with major statistical components. The purpose of the directive was to bring about in each of these departments a consolidation of existing activities into two centers under common leadership, one devoted to the planning and analysis of statistics, and the other devoted to production.

180 YEARS OF CHANGE

Although it is impossible to present a complete record of comparative changes that have taken place in the Bureau during the last 180 years of census taking, Table II represents an effort to show the growth of the decennial census from 1790 to 1970. (It constitutes an updating of a table from *The*

TABLE III

EXPENDITURES FOR MAJOR CLASSES OF WORK DONE
BY THE CENSUS BUREAU, 1947–71

Fiscal Year	Current Statistics (Salaries and Expenses)	Periodic Censuses and Computer Purchases	Work Done for Other Agencies
	Millions of dollars		
1947	11.1	1.4	1.2
1948	7.2	2.2	.5
1949	6.6	8.6	.7
1950	6.8	56.2	1.0
1951	7.0	28.0	1.9
1952	7.0	10.3	3.7
1953	6.9	5.2	3.1
1954	7.3	1.6	2.7
1955	6.2	22.6	2.4
1956	7.3	9.2	2.7
1957	7.4	4.2	4.8
1958	8.2	6.4	5.6
1959	8.6	13.6	5.1
1960	8.6	95.3	6.9
1961	9.6	20.2	7.8
1962	10.7	8.8	11.0
1963	12.8	10.9	12.3
1964	13.6	14.2	11.3
1965	15.1	22.3	12.5
1966	15.7	10.0	18.0
1967	16.4	11.3	24.6
1968	17.1	14.6	28.2
1969	18.1	25.6	23.1
1970	20.1	130.8	22.4
1971	23.2	57.3	26.1

Story of the Census: 1790–1916, published by the Government Printing Office in 1917). In the pre-1902 period, the decennial census included a varying mixture of supplemental inquiries that account for a significant proportion of the total shown. For the 1910–70 period, the data reflect mainly the population, agriculture, and housing censuses.

It might be assumed that the number of enumerators would give the best evidence of changes over the years, but this measure is deceptive, since before 1880 the period of enumeration was longer, and fewer enumerators were involved. The total number of pages in published reports is the best single indicator through 1950, after which the use of high-speed printers and summary tapes renders such data unsuitable for comparative purposes.

Another kind of historical summary is presented in Table III, which shows the annual changes in expenditures for three major subdivisions of work done by the Bureau since 1947: (1) the current program, designated "salaries and expenses," for budgetary purposes, (2) periodic censuses and computer purchases, and (3) work done for other agencies. The greatest change in these three categories has taken place in the volume of work done for other agencies, an increase that reflects legislative provisions for using existing facilities when available as well as the interest of the Office of Management and Budget in making greater use of the Bureau's specialized facilities.

III

Organization and Administration

The Bureau of the Census today is organized primarily along functional lines, as shown in Chart I. The Director of the Bureau, whose authority derives from the Secretary of Commerce, shares the administration of the Bureau with a deputy director. Reporting to the Director, through the deputy director, are five associate directors, offices of public information, of scheduling and control, and of data user services, as well as two special assistants, and a legal adviser at the staff level. The associate directors are each responsible for a group of divisions that plan the content of the various censuses and surveys and the methods of operation, collect the data, perform processing and tabulating, prepare the results for publication, and carry out a variety of supporting functions.

The divisions under two of the associate directors (Demographic Fields and Economic Fields) are concerned mainly with the subject fields in which periodic censuses are taken. Most of the divisions under these two associate directors have a group of subject-matter experts assigned to the planning and execution of the appropriate censuses and surveys. As specialists, they are familiar with the needs of users of census data. They determine which proposals for the collection of

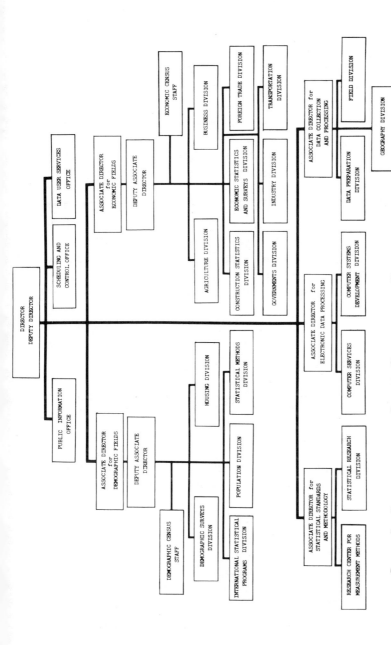

CHART I. BUREAU OF THE CENSUS ORGANIZATION CHART

(*Note*: Administrative and related services are provided by the Office of the Assistant Administrator for Administration, Social and Economic Statistics Administration.)

new data are practical and determine priorities among competing claims. The subject divisions also include specialists in the preparation of procedures, systems design, and computer programs. With the project management responsibilities assigned to them, the subject division personnel become the focal points of a network of operations as the work on a given survey progresses from collection to final publication.

The associate director for Demographic Fields is responsible for two specialized divisions that differ considerably from the subject divisions concerned mainly with particular censuses. One of these is the *International Statistical Programs Division,* which meets the needs of foreign visitors who wish to learn something about U.S. census and statistical activities. Under State Department auspices, this division extends technical services to a number of foreign countries. These services include training of foreign nationals in statistical work as well as advisory assistance to foreign governments through consultants sent abroad. The *Statistical Methods Division* coordinates the application of appropriate statistical techniques in all demographic areas.

The divisions under the associate director for Data Collection and Processing have responsibility for most of the production operations. The *Field Division,* responsible for collections of household data is subject to sharp fluctuations in size, especially when major censuses or surveys are being undertaken and there is a considerable increase in the number of field offices. The Data Preparation Division, located in Jeffersonville, Indiana, provides clerical processing facilities for a wide range of census programs, including card-punching and direct entry devices (encoders) but not computing and tabulating. This division is also responsible for the Personal Census Service Branch, located in Pittsburg, Kansas, which provides information on a fee basis to individuals who request transcripts of their own census records to use as proof of age, citizenship, or relationship in connection with passport applications, pensions, and similar matters. The *Geography Division* provides geographic services required in the Bureau's collection programs.

The divisions and other staff under the associate director for Statistical Standards and Methodology ensure that appropriate statistical methodology and techniques are applied to the fullest extent possible, not only to the Bureau's own censuses and surveys but also to work done for other government agencies. Emphasis is on better methods for statistical operations. Some of this work is done in the *Statistical Research Division* and some by personnel in divisions under other associate directors (such as the Statistical Methods Division in the Demographic Fields area). Persons in the latter category are administratively responsible to their own division but have a direct line of technical responsibility to the Statistical Research Division.

The office of the associate director for Electronic Data Processing is responsible for the maintenance and operation of all computing and tabulating facilities of the Bureau.

The staff offices reporting immediately to the Director include Public Information, Data User Services, and Scheduling and Control offices. The Public Information Office is responsible for the Bureau's relations with the press and other media, and for information programs aimed at segments of the public with which the Bureau works in its various censuses and surveys. The Data User Services Office is responsible for the development of improved systems for the delivery of data to the ultimate user and for the preparation of statistical compendia and special reports covering not only the Bureau's output, but also work of other agencies, both public and private. The Scheduling and Control Office coordinates the planning, scheduling, and execution of the pre- and post-computer processing.

The Bureau receives administrative support and services from the Office of Administration of the Social and Economic

Statistics Administration, a new agency created at the beginning of 1972 in response to the Office of Management and Budget directive referred to in Chapter II. This agency provides budget and finance, personnel, management and organization, administrative services and publication services to both the Census Bureau and the Bureau of Economic Analysis (formerly the Office of Business Economics).

CENTRALIZATION

Until recent years, most of the Bureau's work on a particular census was more or less under the direct control of the chief of the appropriate subject division. The advantages of organization by subject matter are much the same as those which have long been advanced in favor of decentralization of statistical work among a number of agencies. It makes possible a closer relationship between the professional staff and those concerned with data processing and review of tabulations. Communication and coordination are facilitated when both the subject and operating personnel are in a single division. In view of this, the transition from decentralization to a centralized approach has not been rapid.

The first clear-cut example of specialization through centralized operation in the Census Bureau was furnished by machine tabulation. By 1940, the Machine Tabulation Division was serving all parts of the Bureau but the working relationships with the other divisions were close and quite informal. The next move in this direction was the establishment of a Field Division in 1946 to take care of collection work on all the censuses. In the early 1950's, the Economic Operations Division was created to handle all processing work for the 1954 series of economic censuses. The Demographic Operations Division was set up to take care of similar functions for the 1960 Census of Population and Housing. The next move in the evolution of centralization was the consolidation in 1966 of economic and demographic operations to increase the efficiency of large-scale processing.

Organizational changes in 1971 somewhat reduced the degree of centralization in the statistical operations of the Bureau of the Census. The most important change was assigning to the subject-matter division chiefs responsibility for programming and systems design, with the objective of giving them more control over the projects assigned to them, thus making them more immediately accountable for results.

All these changes in recent years have opened the way for the fullest utilization of the electronic computer in statistical system design. Equally important, it has freed subject-matter personnel from most operational tasks—work they have always enjoyed, but which they have not always done efficiently and which has not made the best use of their professional training. As a result of this emancipation, they have more time for analysis and evaluation of the results and for closer relationships with both users and suppliers.

The gains from the technical specialization on the production aspects of statistics have been impressive, even though they have not been well publicized, and large numbers of statisticians are unaware of some of the new developments. Gains from pretabulation processing and from the use of computers to review reported information, to interpolate missing data, and to keep a record of all interpolations have been of extraordinary importance in statistical processing. Centralization also makes for increased flexibility in the use of human and other scarce resources. The staff that has completed the processing on one census or survey can be advantageously shifted to another program as the need arises.

Personnel

The total complement of personnel of the Bureau of the Census consists of those working at the headquarters office in

Washington (actually located in Suitland, Maryland, a suburb located just outside Washington, D.C.), at two field processing centers (Jeffersonville, Indiana; Pittsburg, Kansas), and at twelve data collection centers of the Field Division. Some 3,400 employees at the headquarters office are concerned with most phases of the Bureau's work with the exception of field collection and large-scale processing and card-punching. The flexibility required for the varying work loads of the Bureau are met by the Jeffersonville office and the twelve data collection centers. The work force in the Jeffersonville office drops well below 1,000 at low periods in the ten-year census cycle and rises to 4,000 or 5,000 at the peak of processing activity. The office in Pittsburg, Kansas, with a staff of approximately two hundred, is devoted almost wholly to the search of original census records.

Of the Bureau's professional staff of over one thousand, some two-thirds are statisticians; one-fifth are computer specialists, and the rest are economists, social science analysts, and sociologists. There is a substantial number of accountants, budget analysts, personnel experts, cartographers, management analysts, and systems designers. The permanent clerical and administrative staff does not greatly exceed the number of personnel with professional or other training, but the total clerical force is subject to rapid expansion in the Jeffersonville office, as needed.

The twelve data collection centers of the Field Division have a total of about 200 full-time employees. Interviewers employed on the interim sample surveys of the Bureau normally number about 1,600. Recruited at specific locations, they conduct interviews in any of the 800 counties in the sample for the current population survey. At the time of the population census, the field organization is greatly expanded, with the total number of intermittent workers reaching 160,-000 and the supervisory staff perhaps 15,000.

A detailed description of career opportunities and the Bureau's career development programs will be found in Appendix A.

CHANGES IN WORK LOAD

Chart II shows the over-all changes in work load during the ten-year cycle. All parts of the organization feel the effects of these changes but the greatest impact occurs in a few areas, particularly in the field organization, where the number of intermittent workers may expand by a factor of one hundred within a period of several months. The functions of recruiting, orienting, and training, and record-keeping of all types are subject to enormous changes. In order to cope with the unusual requirements, efforts have been made at different times to utilize programmed learning, television, and recorded lectures illustrated with slides and movies.

The Congress has long recognized that the management of censuses presents many unique problems and has given legislative relief in a number of ways. It has approved changes in the dates of the various censuses, in an effort to even out the work load of the Bureau to the extent possible without undue damage to the needs of census users. The Bureau is given considerable freedom to make use of personnel of other departments, and has been given authority to appoint personnel to temporary positions. The flexibility thus provided to increase and decrease levels of employment rapidly has been most important to the Bureau.

Special authority has been given to provide exemption from competitive Civil Service regulations in connection with the decennial census field appointments of the Bureau. This long-term authority has enabled the Bureau to accomplish extremely sharp expansions and contractions. The use of political sources for candidates for decennial census field work has been a recurrent source of considerable criticism. For example, in 1918 a resolution was presented by the American

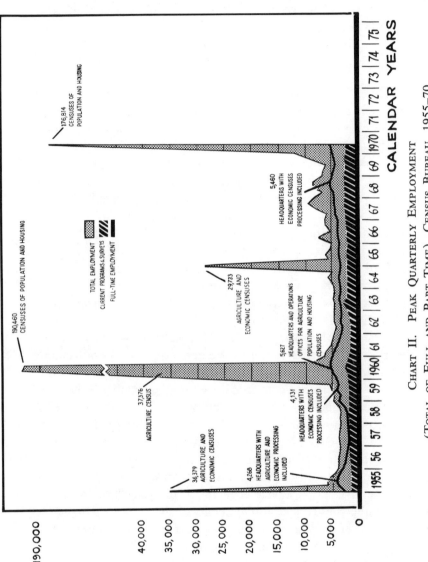

CHART II. PEAK QUARTERLY EMPLOYMENT
(TOTAL OF FULL AND PART TIME), CENSUS BUREAU, 1955–70

Statistical Association, calling attention to the importance of the forthcoming 1920 census and urging that the appointments of both supervisors and enumerators be taken out of political hands. The association asked that supervisors be appointed through an agency of the Civil Service Commission. In 1954, the report of the Intensive Review Committee, appointed by the Secretary of Commerce to review the programs of the Bureau of the Census, referred to political procedures as "the legacy of an outmoded past" and strongly urged that use be made of the public employment office in carrying out the necessary recruitment.

The task of assembling a large field organization at comparatively low rates of pay for a short period of time is a difficult one at best. In any event, for a number of reasons, the difficulties arising from political influence today are less than in earlier times. With the broader understanding of the key importance of the decennial census, it has been possible to convince congressmen and political officials that tests and other criteria for the selection of field staff are absolutely essential. Hence, in recent censuses, the Bureau has been able to avoid accepting unsuitable candidates. In many cases, capable professional and managerial people have been willing to take temporary census supervisory jobs in response to appeals made through political channels. The number of conventional supervisory appointments was somewhat reduced in 1970. Special offices managed by career people were set up in a number of large cities, where the problems of carrying out the census were so great as to require personnel with previous census experience. A final factor reducing the importance of this issue is that the size of the staff to be recruited will continue to decrease as more and more of the census collection work is carried out on a mail basis. With these changes it is to be hoped that this issue, which always receives more critical attention outside the Bureau than it deserves, will gradually fade away.

IV

Censuses—Major and Minor

By far the best-known function of the Bureau of the Census is the taking of periodic censuses. Indeed, this activity so overshadows all others in the public mind that employees of the Bureau have long been exposed to the quips of friends who assume that census workers have little to do except during the first year or two of each decade.

The Bureau's series of censuses have been referred to as "the mirror of America." The metaphor is an apt one, since periodic inventories of people and their institutions provide an unrivaled depiction of some of the most important elements of our human and material resources.

Table IV presents the gradual evolution, from 1790 to 1970, of the present mix of major censuses. It is limited to those areas of inquiry that are still pursued. It departs somewhat from the terminology used in the legislative provisions for the early censuses. Typically, inquiries relating to such subjects as manufactures, agriculture, and mining were not specifically designated as censuses before 1902. They were merely specified as subjects of inquiry for a particular decennial census, and special or supplementary schedules were developed for carrying out such inquiries.

In Table IV, the first column (Population) reflects the fact that this census has the longest record of the entire series and is the only one strictly uniform in its timing. The population census enjoys another distinction—that of being the only statistical activity specifically provided for in the Constitution and required for the decennial reapportionment of seats in the House of Representatives. This has not been an unmixed blessing. At the outset, it was certainly a source of prestige for the new activity and contributed to the willingness of Congress to make reporting mandatory and to impose, for failure to comply, a penalty of $20, a significant amount in those days. However, it has provided strict constructionists of the Constitution an opportunity to argue against expanding the scope of the census ever since 1850, when Southern members of Congress quoted the Constitution in an effort to reduce the scope of the census. Francis A. Walker, one of the outstanding Superintendents of the Census, referred to this conflict in an article published in January, 1888, in the *Quarterly Journal of Economics:*

> Personally, a strict constructionist, I do not believe the Constitution has been outgrown; but I do believe that the American people have outgrown the little, paltry, bigoted construction of the Constitution which, in 1850, questioned in Congress the right of the people of the United States to learn whatever they might please to know regarding their own numbers, condition, and resources. It has become simply absurd to hold any longer that a government which has a right to tax any and all the products of agriculture and manufactures, to supervise the making and selling of butterine, to regulate the agencies of transportation, to grant public moneys to schools and colleges, to conduct agricultural experiments and distribute seeds and plant-cuttings all over the United States, to institute scientific surveys by land and deep soundings at sea, has not full authority to pursue any branch of statistical information which may conduce to wise legislation, intelligent administration, or equitable taxation, or in any other way promote the general welfare.

TABLE IV

MAJOR CONTINUING CENSUSES, 1790–1970

Year	Population	Manufactures	Agriculture	Mineral Industries	Governments	Business	Housing	Construction	Transportation
1790	X								
1800	X								
1810	X	X							
1820	X	X							
1830	X								
1840	X	X	X	X [a]	X				
1850	X	X	X	X [a]	X				
1860	X	X	X	X [a]	X				
1870	X	X	X	X	X				
1880	X	X	X	X					
1890	X	X	X	X					
1900	X	X	X						
1902				X					
1905		X			X				
1910	X	X	X	X					
1912					X				
1915		X							
1920	X	X	X	X					
1921		X							
1922					X				
1923		X							

Year									
1925		X							
1927		X	X						
1929		X							
1930	X	X		X	X		X	X	
1931		X							
1932				X					
1933		X		X	X				
1935		X			X			X	
1937		X							
1939		X							
1940	X	X		X	X		X	X	
1942				X		X			
1945		X		X					
1947		X							
1948		X			X	X			
1950	X	X		X	X		X		
1954		X		X	X				
1955		X^{b}							
1957				X					
1958	X	X		X	X	X	X		
1960		X^{b}		X	X	X	X		
1962				X					
1963		X^{b}		X	X		X		
1965								X	X
1967		X			X		X	X	X
1970		X^{b}		X	X	X	X	X	X

a Included under the general schedule of industry for these years. b Taken in fall of preceding year.

Since Walker's day, the right of Congress to authorize the collection of various types of statistical data has been tested many times in the federal courts. Nevertheless, despite the specific language of the court decisions and the increased awareness of the importance of census data to public and private decision-makers, there was much sympathy in Congress for the point of view of the strict constructionists in the years 1968 and 1969, when plans were being made for the 1970 census.

EVOLUTION OF POPULATION INQUIRIES

Selected highlights in the evolution of the census of population over the years 1790 to 1970 are shown in Table V.

TABLE V

HISTORICAL HIGHLIGHTS OF THE CENSUS OF POPULATION,
1790–1970

1790 — Institution of the world's first periodic population enumeration.

1830 — Introduction of printed schedules of uniform size.

1850 — Enumeration of each member of family by name.
Central tabulation of results in Washington.

1880 — Enumeration directed by supervisors of census rather than by assistants to the marshals.
Confidentiality pledge included in enumerators' oaths.
Time limits on enumeration: two weeks in cities of 10,000, one month elsewhere.

1890 — First use of electric tabulating system.
Collection of data on unemployed.

1900 — All employees required to observe confidentiality provisions.

1910 — Clerical jobs filled by competitive examinations.

1940 — Introduction of sampling.
Introduction of income inquiries and labor force approach.

1960 — Extensive use of self-enumeration.

1970 — Mail-out/mail-back approach in larger metropolitan areas.

In the first six censuses, 1790–1840, the methods of enumeration and summarization remained much the same.

Through 1830, the number of inquiries was relatively small, even though they regularly went somewhat beyond the minimum number required to meet the Constitutional provision for establishing the distribution of membership in the House of Representatives. The departures from the minimum were probably not sufficient to disturb the strict constructionists of that day. In 1840, however, there was a significant extension of the scope of the enumeration to a level that continued in the next three censuses. For the first time, information was collected on occupations—a development quite consistent with the collection of information pertaining to manufacturing and other activities of the young nation. By the 1840's, free public schools were becoming more common throughout the North and the principle of equal educational opportunity was gaining acceptance. This development was in line with the addition of literacy as an item of inquiry in 1840.

The censuses of 1850 to 1870 marked a significant change in the quality of population censuses in this country, a development growing out of the complaints following the 1840 census—an enlarged undertaking that proved much too difficult for procedures that had changed little since 1790. The most important feature was, perhaps, the considerably greater attention given to the census form, which for the first time made separate provisions for each member of the household. This, together with the central tabulation of the results in Washington, made possible much more significant tabulations of the results of the census. Another great improvement was the establishment of the position of Superintending Clerk of the Census, an official reporting directly to the Secretary of the Interior. The inquiries in the 1850–70 period reflected the continuation of the interest shown in education, social problems, and economic progress. For example, a question on school attendance was added in 1850. Concern over social problems was reflected in various inquiries concerning several classes of the handicapped, such as the blind, the deaf, the insane, and persons classified as idiots. Evidence of interest in measuring economic progress was shown in the census of 1850, with its inquiry regarding real estate, and in 1860 and 1870, when the value of personal estates was also required. (There was then no legislative provision requiring confidentiality of returns.)

In the 1880 and 1890 censuses, the nation established a record with respect to the number and variety of inquiries. In previous censuses there had never been more than five or six broad schedules of inquiry in the decennial census—population, agriculture, industry, mining, and the like—but in 1880 and in 1890 there were more than 200 general and special schedules relating to many different topics and including some 13,000 separate inquiries or details. Although only a relatively small number of the questions pertained to the general population, both years were remarkable for the proliferation of questions pertaining to defective and handicapped individuals. As evidence of the amount of detail on these subjects, we can refer to the special report on persons classified as idiots in the 1880 census. In the tabulation of causes of idiocy, we find one cause given as "drinking cold water" and another, "rocking and swinging." One particularly detailed table included in this category a person with a large head who could do skilled labor but could not articulate and could not walk. Needless to say, the special report is a rich source of what families reported about their defective members.

In the census of 1900, the last of the censuses under the temporary census organization, there was a marked reduction from the scope of the 1890 enumeration. The early completion of the 1900 census was attributed to the fact that the census was limited to four subjects—population, mortality, agriculture, and manufactures. Other subjects were to be covered after the completion of the decennial inquiry.

Population censuses since the establishment of a permanent Bureau of the Census in 1902 have reflected a significant, but not uninterrupted growth in the scope and number of questions concerning our population, as more and more government programs have related to aspects of our social and economic life. Thus in 1940, questions on labor force activity, on income, and internal migration revealed the special concern of a nation that had suffered from prolonged depression and still had large numbers of unemployed and displaced workers. The increased emphasis upon fertility inquiries was due to the continued decline of rates of population increase. The addition of questions on place of work and means of transportation in 1960 indicated an effort to meet some of the problems arising from increased concentration of the population in urban areas. Fortunately the introduction and rapid expansion of statistical sampling over the period 1940 to 1970 made it possible to cover new subjects without adding to the burden of response borne by the average household.

New Censuses, 1810–40: Manufactures, Agriculture, Mining

Only 20 years after the introduction of the census of population, the nation turned its attention to the first of a series of inquiries that would eventually describe most of the country's economic institutions and activities. Although the early measures of productive and extractive industries were open to much criticism, they had indicated something about the variety and importance of the economy of a young nation.

In view of the great emphasis that our nation has always placed upon production, it is not surprising that the first three inquiries added to the decennial census were connected with physical production—manufacturing in 1810, and agriculture and mining in 1840. Table IV shows not only that manufacturing is the oldest of the inquiries, next to population, but also that it accounts for the largest number of individual censuses. It was the first major census on a five-year basis under the 1902 Act establishing a permanent Bureau of the Census. It was also the first and only census to be put on a two-year basis—a pattern that continued from 1921 to 1939. In 1948, when it was returned to a five-year basis, specific assurance had to be given that the annual sample survey of manufactures would meet some of the needs for information that had previously been available every two years.

The introduction of questions on manufacturing in 1810 took place at a time when this activity was quite limited in size and scope. The content of inquiries concerned with production has, of course, expanded greatly over the years. Although information was collected in 1810 only on the kind, quantity, and value of goods manufactured, by the time of the second inquiry in 1820 the census had already been broadened to include capital investment, contingent expenses, numbers of persons employed, wage payments, and quantity and value of materials used, as well as the quantity and kind of machinery used. The results were apparently quite unsatisfactory, and the inquiry on manufactures was not repeated in 1830. The year 1840, which marked a significant increase in the scope of the population census, also marked the resumption of inquiries on manufacturing and the institution of inquiries relating to agriculture and mining. President Van Buren, in his second annual message to Congress on December 8, 1838, not only recommended the adoption of the necessary legislation for taking the sixth census, but also raised a question as to "whether the scope of the measure might not be usefully extended by causing it to embrace authentic statistical returns of the great interests specially intrusted to or necessarily affected by the legislation of Congress." Shortly after this, in 1839, Archibald Russell brought out a book entitled, *Principles of Statistical Inquiry as Illustrated in Proposals for Uniting an Examination Into the Resources of the United States With the Census to be Taken in 1840*. It was part of Russell's argument that agriculture, manufacturing, and other fields could be enumerated along with the 1840 Census of Population.

The early censuses of production were handicapped by lack of public acceptance and by the discontinuities inherent in the fact that the work was performed by a series of temporary organizations. The year 1850 was one of significant change in the quality of the periodic censuses for manufactures, as well as for population. As shown in Table VI, this is the

TABLE VI

HISTORICAL HIGHLIGHTS OF THE CENSUS OF MANUFACTURES,
1810–1967

1810 —	Introduction of series.
1850 —	Institution of penalty for failure to respond.
	Assurance given of confidential treatment of returns.
	Central tabulation of results.
1880 —	Use of special agents to collect data in areas of industrial concentration.
1890 —	Expanded report on motive power, including electric motors.
1900 —	Exclusion of hand industries.
1905 —	Beginning of five-year censuses of manufactures.
	First use of collection by mail from some manufacturers.
1921 —	Beginning of two-year censuses of manufactures.
1947 —	First major census to be collected almost completely by mail.
1948 —	Return to five-year schedule.
1954 —	Collection of extensive data on water use.
1967 —	Elimination of small employers from census of manufactures; data collected from tax records.

year in which a penalty was imposed upon firms that refused to respond. The penalty, coupled with the assurance that the returns would receive confidential treatment, led to a much more nearly complete response by manufacturers. Thanks to the greater attention to the schedules—the work of a newly created interagency board—the inquiries covered the most important phases of manufacturing: labor, energy, and commodity detail. Finally, the tabulations were carried out centrally in Washington for the first time, and the resulting body of data provided the beginnings of a historical series that has been carried down to the present. In the process, the details of the censuses of manufactures have increased greatly, and some significant changes have been introduced. For example, a specific inquiry on value added by manufacturing was included in 1904, and another on man-hours of production workers in 1933.

The censuses of extractive industries (agriculture and mining) resemble the census of manufacturing in the requirement of detailed information on inputs and outputs. The successive inquiries used in the census of agriculture tell the story of the transition from small family farms to larger and larger commercial enterprises having more of the characteristics of corporate business. With this transition, there has been increased emphasis on economic organization and equipment, on financial characteristics, and on specialized farms and agricultural services. With the greater emphasis upon agriculture as a business, the 1969 census was based upon a mailing list derived from administrative records, similar to those used for manufactures, trade, and services.

CENSUS OF GOVERNMENTS

The origins of this census are to be found in the schedule of inquiries relating to social statistics. Beginning in 1850, data were collected regarding taxes and public debt, as well as crime, pauperism, public libraries, newspapers and periodicals, religion, wages, and prices. The reason for the social statistics schedule is to be found in the growing concern with social problems, as indicated by the fact that the population census included inquiries regarding the handicapped and the defective, as well as questions regarding school attendance and literacy.

Of the long list of subjects in the schedule for social statistics, the only ones that became a part of the nation's series of continuing censuses are those pertaining to taxation, expenditures, and debts. In the years 1850 to 1870, there was much interest in the wealth of the growing nation, and the inquiries were chiefly concerned with assessed valuations as an indication of wealth and with state and local taxation. Later in the century, increasing emphasis was placed upon measuring public indebtedness. In the twentieth century, the census of governments has undergone an occasional expansion to develop national estimates of wealth. It has been modified, with some fluctuations in scope, to provide information decennially (and since 1957 quinquennially) on organization and structure of state and local governments, public employment, tax property values, and governmental finance. The marked growth in revenues, expenditures, and employment of state and local governments has given this series of censuses a value that was not apparent at its inauguration. A similar broadening tendency can be noted in recent program planning. The government census inquiries are being expanded to provide a contribution to criminal statistics in the form of data on numbers, activities, and payrolls for persons engaged in various phases of law enforcement.

CENSUS OF BUSINESS

The first census of trade and services was undertaken in 1930, more than one hundred years after the first inquiries relating to manufactures. Some explanation of the reasons for the new activity is contained in an appraisal of census programs made in 1954 by a group of marketing experts requested to advise the Secretary of Commerce. They referred to the fact that the need for census data in the field of marketing became apparent around 1920, when U.S. industry was beginning to develop methods of mass distribution.

The recognition of the needs for marketing facts was due in considerable measure to the fact that Herbert Hoover, Secretary of Commerce from 1921 to 1928, was much interested in promoting both domestic and foreign trade. The censuses of retail trade, wholesale trade, and services were taken at irregular intervals in the 1930's, partly with the assistance of unemployment relief funds. In 1948, when new census legislation was enacted as Public Law 671, the census of business was placed on a five-year basis for the first time. In recent years, the censuses of business, manufactures, and mineral industries have been taken for years ending in 2 and 7 and are often referred to as the economic censuses.

Censuses of construction were taken as part of the censuses of business (1930, 1935, 1939), but enumerators were unable to identify considerable numbers of those operating in this industry, and the results were never well accepted. By 1967, when the series of construction censuses was resumed, it was possible to use mailing lists based upon administrative records and thereby achieve significantly more satisfactory coverage of contractors whose places of business were often not readily recognizable by an enumerator.

HOUSING AND TRANSPORTATION

Despite fragmentary early information relating to housing, such as tenure and mortgage status, the first census on this subject was provided by congressional enactment in 1940, shortly before the census was to start. A few years earlier there had been a collapse of real estate prices, with severe losses to financial institutions, depositors, and homeowners. By the end of the decade an extensive amount of housing legislation had been enacted in recognition of President Franklin Roosevelt's repeated references to the ill-housed. There was likewise strong support from business interests, who realized that information regarding the characteristics of housing in different areas would be a valuable tool for market analysis. For the decades after 1940, the importance of statistics on our housing inventory was reflected in the passage of a number of acts, whose formulation made specific use of many of the statistics included in the decennial census of housing.

The latest of the current series of major censuses is the census of transportation, first taken in 1963, although Public Law 671 authorized and required this census on a five-year basis in 1948. The fifteen-year period of inactivity was due to a variety of factors. A census in this field is unusually difficult because it must be set up in such a way as to avoid duplicating information publicly available from federal regulatory bodies. In view of this, as well as the diverse nature of the activities to be covered, the census of transportation took a form quite different from that of any other periodic census. The major parts are a truck inventory and use survey, a national travel survey to measure the volume and characteristics of individual and household travel, and a commodity transportation survey to measure commodity shipments for major classes of shippers.

Uses of Census Data

Statistics provided by the periodic censuses are unique among government statistics with respect to the variety of users and applications of the data. In the words of a distinguished demographer, the late Samuel Stouffer:

> The products of the Bureau of the Census are like the oxygen in the air. They are consumed so widely that they are accepted as a matter of course and are so often used after analysis and interpretation by one or more intermediaries that the user does not readily recognize their source.

This universality of use is not surprising when we realize that the data gathered by the Bureau cover all U.S. inhabitants, the homes they live in, the factories and service trades that account for their total supply of goods and services, the farms and mines producing foods, fibers, fuels, and other commodities, and the retail and wholesale trade establishments that provide the flow of goods to ultimate consumers. Knowledge about some or all of these statistical universes is essential to decisions involved in planning, administration, and evaluation—regardless of whether the decisions are to be made by government, by business, or by nonprofit organizations. There are, of course, major difficulties in identifying, listing, and evaluating all these uses. The importance of a particular use is difficult to measure, and the exact role played by an individual figure is often unknown. The nature of the uses varies from one census to another.

Uses of Population and Housing Census Data

The primarily demographic censuses—population and housing—have a particular pattern of use because population is the source of the labor force. The classification of uses can take many forms, depending upon the particular interests of the classifier. One system, which is reasonably compact and understandable although not free of duplication, classifies the uses under four headings, which are applicable whether we are considering government, business, or nonprofit organizations: (1) research and planning, (2) measuring potential demand, (3) determining sites for production or service facilities, and (4) administration and evaluation of results.

1. In applications pertaining to research and planning, we find that the projections of trends of various sorts, including complex relationships, have provided the basis for important government and business policies. The study of factors associated with population developments may be very important for future plans. Legislative hearings and reviews frequently use census statistics extensively as a basis for legislative

changes. Many of the decisions of local governments with respect to such issues as housing, education, and crime depend directly upon data from the population and housing censuses.

2. The potential demands for many kinds of services and goods are reflected in census statistics, both for total population and for particular subgroups. Such figures reveal needs for programs relating to urban renewal, adult education, recreational facilities, youth and senior citizen activities, and highway planning. Among the examples of business use are the applications of census data to determine future loads for utilities. The numbers in particular age and sex groups are often directly related to the marketing of such products as cereals, beer, and toys. By using a combination of population and housing characteristics, very specific measures of particular markets can be derived.

3. A third use of census data is to determine locations for various kinds of facilities. Local governments have recurrent need for such information in connection with public housing, schools, hospitals, libraries, settlement houses, and many other facilities. Examples of similar use by business relate to the location of shopping centers, branch banks, manufacturing plants, new units of chain stores, and units for wholesale distribution.

4. A number of quite different uses can be cited when we come to administration and evaluation of results. Well-known examples in the government field are the apportionment of seats in the Congress, the establishment of districts for state legislatures, the distribution of funds at all levels, the granting of licenses, and the determination of the numbers and salaries of local officials in a number of states. Business uses of the administrative type include decisions regarding territories of salesmen, amounts spent on advertising, the bases for service charges (as in radio and television usage), and the carrying out of market surveys to determine customer attitudes.

Uses of Data from Economic Censuses

The nation's series of economic censuses, of which manufactures is the oldest and perhaps the best known, are of central importance for many of the decisions made by government and by the business establishments that account for a very large proportion of our gross national product. In the case of manufacturing establishments, the amount of detail is very extensive, including the kinds of materials they consume, the labor they employ, capital requirements, and an indication of whether the product is for home use, further manufacturing, or for capital use. Over the years, our government policies relating to the encouragement of capital investment, the conservation of resources, the restriction of monopolies, and the encouragement of foreign trade have often depended on information from the economic censuses. The government's interest derives in part from the fact that it is an important buyer of the products of industry. Moreover, many of the nation's indexes relating to national product and the level of industrial production depend upon bench marks provided by the periodic censuses.

The basic decisions of businessmen are likewise dependent upon information regarding our aggregate productive and distributive activity. The great variety of commodities and complexity of manufacturing processes make it ever more essential for business to have comprehensive facts for its guidance. For individual companies, the censuses provide information which can help them determine where they should locate new plants or sales offices, as well as when they should modify facilities or make use of different materials. Business firms make extensive use of the censuses as an indication of what other companies in their fields are doing.

The data contained in the censuses are a gold mine for research into the interrelationships among manufacturing and distributing establishments. The trends and relationships revealed by such research provide the bases for many kinds of operating decisions. The relationships among industries are so complex and difficult to summarize that firms are continually faced with the need for information regarding those that supply goods for their use and those that are customers. The detailed input/output tables of this kind of information depend very largely upon the storehouse of data available from the economic censuses.

MINOR CENSUSES

Over most of the period during which the program of censuses has been evolving, there has been a quite variable series of minor censuses, involving coverage of a particular class of individuals or institutions on a periodic basis. Up to 1902 these inquiries were uniformly decennial, but since then they have been carried out at various intervals during the decade. The range of subjects is suggested by the following selection: fish and fisheries, commerce, unemployment, mortality, religion, insurance, trade societies, real estate mortgages, electric railways, central electric light and power stations, and telephones and telegraphs. The most interesting item in this list is religion, which was really a special inquiry addressed to religious bodies from 1850 to 1890 and which, in the 1902 Act, became a regular though not mandatory census. Censuses of religious bodies were conducted decennially from 1906 to 1936. In 1946, money was provided to start this census, but the funds necessary to complete it were later denied. Subsequently, despite some efforts to obtain funds, there has been no resumption of the series, and it seems safe to predict that the 1936 report will remain the final one in this series.

The collection of statistics on crime is an example of an activity that has come full circle as far as government attention is concerned. Such data were first collected as a part of the decennial program in 1850 and received increasing emphasis during the remainder of the nineteenth century. In the 1940's, however, the last portions of the field of criminal and judicial statistics were transferred to the Department of Justice, but the authorization for collection remained in census legislation. Late in the 1960's, the needs for better statistics in this area were recognized and the services of the Bureau were called upon by the Justice Department to help in the development of a considerably increased program.

Small Area Data

A unique merit of the periodic censuses is their ability to provide data for very small geographic areas. In earlier years these areas were limited to states, counties and subdivisions of counties, towns, villages, and other areas with boundaries fixed by local ordinance. Then, in 1910, through the efforts of Dr. Walter Laidlaw of New York City, the Bureau started to provide data for small subdivisions of cities (census tracts) to study neighborhoods smaller than boroughs or wards. The census tract program was expanded sharply after 1910 and eventually was applied to all metropolitan areas.

In the 1960's, even more flexible programs were needed, particularly programs that could be used to provide summaries for areas conforming to special subdivisions in various cities. Through the use of computerized mailing lists and computerized coordinates to identify corners of blocks, the way has been opened for a very great increase in the ability to provide small area data on a custom basis and to provide computer maps as needed.

Another feature of the census program has been the development of special statistical areas in recognition of the fact that central cities by themselves have long since lost their original economic and social significance. For many kinds of analysis the population in central cities must be combined with that in surrounding areas to provide aggregates significant for research in labor force and housing, as well as for many kinds of market and community planning. The first attack on this problem took place in the 1940 census with the creation of *metropolitan districts,* which included central cities and surrounding areas selected primarily on the basis of population density. Such areas proved difficult for other agencies to use and, accordingly, *standard metropolitan statistical areas* were adopted for the 1950 census. Outside of New England, these areas were uniformly composed of entire counties selected on the basis of their close relationship to the central cities.

The *urbanized area* was instituted by the Census Bureau in 1950 as a means of better separating the urban and rural population in the vicinity of cities of 50,000 or more. The urbanized area is defined as consisting of the central city plus the adjacent built-up area constituting the *urban fringe.* The criteria for inclusion in the fringe are somewhat complex, but the intention is to include areas settled densely enough to have the block pattern characteristic of urban concentrations.

TECHNICAL ADVANCES DUE TO CENSUSES

One of the important contributions of the periodic censuses is the impetus they have given to a long series of technical advances, which will be described in subsequent chapters. It has proved possible, and highly desirable, to use a small percentage of the census funds as a means of improving statistical technology in a number of directions. For example, the conversion from canvassing to collection by mail in the several censuses involved experimental work and testing for more than two decades. The use of administrative records for mailing lists and for certain kinds of data likewise involved research for a considerable number of years. Most of the special equipment used in the Census Bureau could not have been developed except for the resources provided by the major censuses and, finally, the developments in sampling and response research were greatly speeded up by the opportunities available only in the larger censuses. It is somewhat ironic that funds justified for the censuses provided the base for advances in statistical methods and technology that have paved the way for a major shift in relative emphasis away from the periodic censuses.

V

Current Statistics

"Current statistics," for the purposes of this chapter, include statistics generated by all programs of the Bureau of the Census except the periodic censuses described in the last chapter.

The two major components of current statistics are intercensal statistics (collected between periods of regular census taking) and foreign trade statistics. The former, accounting for some 80 per cent of the current statistics total, consists of annual, quarterly, monthly, and even weekly, series of data, and provides information on changes between the five- and ten-year bench marks furnished by the periodic censuses. Most of the intercensal statistics programs are relatively new, having been established since World War II. They may be regarded as a direct response to the growing demand for up-to-date information for decision-making by government and by private industry.

Foreign trade statistics, on the other hand, are not related to the periodic censuses and represent one of the oldest statistical activities of the federal government. The first Congress provided for such statistics, and the Treasury Department began keeping a record of foreign trade in 1789. Foreign trade statistics are based upon the official documents used for recording exports and imports and, therefore, involve no canvassing or collecting activity.

TYPES OF INTERCENSAL STATISTICS

The earliest means of providing intercensal information applying to population involved the simple mathematical extension of figures from the latest census or series of censuses. Requiring no data collection activity, it was rapid and cheap but of little use at times of rapid change in growth rates.

Substantially improved measures of population change became possible with the rapid growth of vital registration systems in the first three decades of this century. The current figures on births and deaths provided for the nation and for most states a new and powerful tool for bettering the old-style estimates of population change. More recently, the administrative records from state and local school systems, the Social Security Administration, and the Immigration and Naturalization Service have made possible increasingly detailed and sophisticated population estimates and projections.

Most of the expansion of intercensal statistics in the past thirty years has been provided by surveys based upon samples of the universes covered by the periodic censuses. The samples in most cases have been drawn from the entire statistical universe, but in some cases they are limited to a particular segment. In the case of a survey of a particular industry, the number of establishments is sometimes so small that it may be feasible to cover all or most of the units on an annual, or even more frequent, basis. With the advance of statistical technology, the sample designs for a number of major intercensal programs have gone through a series of dramatic changes.

As early as 1888, Francis A. Walker called attention to the need for intercensal statistics. He was the first Superintendent of the Census to recognize clearly the need for informing the public regarding the shortcomings of census data. Fifty years elapsed before there was really much progress in the direction envisioned by Walker. The most probable reasons for this delay were: (1) the lack of general recognition of a need great enough to justify major outlays in this direction, (2) the absence of explicit legislative authorization, and (3) the need for the creation of statistical technology appropriate for the new task. These developments took place more or less concurrently, with the progress in one area helping to encourage advances elsewhere.

The report of the War Industries Board after World War I referred to the need for statistics on the production and flow of important industrial commodities. A beginning in providing such information was made in the 1920's, but in the early 1930's, prolonged depression led to retrenchment in various lines of statistical work. By the time of World War II, the need for current statistics had become acute, and the War Production Board transferred substantial sums to the Census Bureau during each of the final three years of the war. Three years after the termination of the war, when legislation was introduced to provide specific authorization for an intercensal statistical program, it was strongly supported by business groups. Clearly, by that date, the need for current data for current decision-making was well recognized, and there was ample justification for the development of a program of intercensal statistics.

A second requirement for such development was specific legislative authority. Although the 1929 Census Act represented an important advance in a number of respects, it contained no specific provision for interim or current surveys. The only basis for such surveys was the executive authority of the Secretary of Commerce under the Organic Act establishing the Department. Such general powers were adequate for an occasional activity to provide current statistical intelligence, but they had at least two weaknesses as a support for a comprehensive program. First, they furnished no assurance of congressional support, and it was necessary for the Secretary to make a specific determination of need in advance of every survey. Second, there was no mandatory authority in support of the collection of the interim data, a deficiency that would seriously affect the ability of the Bureau to make a complete collection of some kinds of data.

These problems were solved by the passage of Public Law 671 (see Chapter II). The mandatory authority for collecting annual data of the type included in censuses was supported by business because of the recognition that lack of response by even a few large establishments would greatly impair the value of the statistics. The inauguration of an annual survey of manufactures at the time of the new legislation was in accordance with the agreement of business users to forgo the two-year census of manufactures if a new annual sample could be provided.

The third, and most important, factor facilitating a program of intercensal statistics was the development of statistical technology and the establishment of an organization for carrying out such work. The intensive research and development which began in the early 1940's will be described in a later chapter. As a result of this program, dramatic gains were made in the sophistication and reliability of sampling procedures appropriate for current statistics in various fields. The costs, however, remained high enough to limit severely the number of areas for which statistical information could be provided at reasonable outlays.

Current Business Reports

Even though domestic trade was one of the last fields to be covered by a decennial census, it was the first to have an intercensal survey based upon the full universe of the census. Both developments are to be explained in terms of the recognition by marketers of the growing need for measures of market potentials, as well as for statistics on the distribution of consumer expenditures throughout the United States. By the mid-1930's, the efforts of the Bureau of Foreign and Domestic Commerce and of the Census Bureau had led to the development of a monthly series of retail trade statistics and later to the initiation of an annual survey of retail trade. The roles of the two bureaus were not clearly differentiated at the outset, but in 1939 an agreement was reached, under which the Census Bureau would collect, publish, and release basic tables on current statistics of retail and wholesale trade and manufacturing, while the Bureau of Foreign and Domestic Commerce would analyze and interpret the data and publish such interpretations.

The early samples of retail and wholesale establishments were based upon a continuing panel of firms. Because they were not probability samples, the calculation of sampling errors was not possible. Biases showed up in the series because the sample was not representative of small firms, and it was not feasible to ensure coverage of newly created enterprises.

During the 1940's extensive research was conducted to provide the basis for efficient probability samples representing the full census universe. The utilization of area sampling made it possible for the first time to sample retail businesses by probability methods. The field organization created in 1946 provided a mechanism for administration of an area sample distributed widely enough to be an efficient and appropriate probability sample but with sufficient clustering to make collection possible without undue cost. With the new sample, begun in 1951, there were produced not only month-to-month trend data but also dollar volume estimates. Additions to the survey in the next few years included estimates of monthly inventories, monthly accounts receivable balances, and weekly retail figures.

In the late 1960's it became apparent that records available from the Social Security Administration and the Internal Revenue Service could be utilized as the basis of the current sample for retail trade statistics. Since 1954 these lists had been used in taking the censuses of business, and the experience provided assurance that this procedure could be applied to the current sample. Furthermore, the increasingly sophisticated electronic equipment used for maintenance of the Social Security and Revenue Service records made it feasible to depend upon the records to reveal turnover due to sales of businesses, to mergers, new incorporations, and resumption of operations by firms temporarily closed down. Since firms without employees are not included in the Social Security Administration's file of employers, a small-size area sample was retained to reveal the changes in operations of small units without paid employees as well as deficiencies in the lists caused by slippages in the mechanism for keeping them up to date. It was anticipated that the replacement of most of the area sample by a list sample carried out wholly by mail would considerably reduce the cost of the retail trade series. The list sample thus opened up the possibility for more area and commodity detail with the same total outlay, and also provided a flexible means for setting up a sample to reflect the characteristics of a special kind of business. Furthermore, the list sample ensures a closer relationship than ever before between the surveys and the periodic censuses of retail trade, since both are based upon the same lists. For the same reason, the intercensal statistics are also more closely related to any data derived from administrative records, as, for example, the County Business Patterns described later on in this chapter.

The foregoing description of the current business statistics program has been solely in terms of the retail trade segment, which is much larger than the wholesale trade and the service trade segments. The evolution of intercensal statistics in these other two fields has gone through a series of developments similar to those described for retail trade.

Current Statistics of Manufacturing

The field of manufacturing differs markedly from that of trade and services with respect to intercensal statistics. The much smaller number of establishments and the greater concentration of activity in a comparatively small number of very large units make it feasible to sample the lists without supplementation by an area sample. In the case of some segments of manufacturing, it is possible to cover all of the units or at least all above a fairly low cutoff point.

The need for annual or more frequent measures led initially to surveys of important areas, such as lumber and textile fibers. Statistics from such surveys gave companies information on the rate of growth of their industries, on new investments and inventories, and on shipments, materials used, and other elements important in company management. Thus, the policies of individual companies could be continually adjusted in the light of new information made available by the periodic series of data on particular commodities. Even more important was the use made of the series in the analysis of economic conditions, the measurement of productivity, and the determination of appropriate governmental policies.

Although some of these surveys antedated by twenty years or more the establishment of a series of monthly retail trade reports, they were initiated for quite specialized industrial needs, and they covered so little of the full range of manufacturing that they could scarcely be regarded as intercensal statistics.

The field of current industrial reports showed no major growth until World War II. Within twenty years, the number grew to about 120 different annual, quarterly, or monthly surveys, the selection being based upon the size of an industry, its strategic importance, the cost of collection, and the need for information in addition to that already available from the census or other sources. In a few industries, the data were based upon probability samples, but in most cases either the full list of establishments was covered or all but those below a fairly low cutoff point. The processing of the current industrial reports has been carried out on a highly automatic basis. Among the features of this system are computer-generated forms and automatic check-in, editing, correction, imputation, analysis, and printing of copy for offset reproduction.

The annual survey of manufactures, based on a probability sample of about 65,000 manufacturing establishments, was the first survey designed to provide intercensal data for all manufacturing industries. Unlike the current industrial reports, which provide information on many specific commodities, this survey yields data for industry groups and value of shipments for product classes. It also furnishes a number of key measures for manufacturing such as employment, payroll, man-hours, value added by manufacture, capital outlays, and inventories. By virtue of its coverage of all of the large firms and a substantial fraction of the smaller ones, the annual survey of manufactures yields data for states, SMSA's (Standard Metropolitan Statistical Areas), and large counties.

A noteworthy by-product of the annual survey is a large number of time series of individual establishment reports for some twenty years. Analysis of these series reveals patterns of growth in different industries and yields objective evidence on capacity utilization.

The intercensal program in the field of manufacturing also includes two comprehensive monthly surveys: manufacturers' shipments, orders, and inventories; and manufacturers' export sales and orders. The first is based upon a panel of about 3,500 companies representing all types of manufacturing, while the second is limited to durable goods producers. These surveys yield only a limited amount of industrial detail, but they have proved extremely useful in giving current data on industrial developments that promote an understanding of business conditions and prospects. They serve not only as strategic economic indicators but also improve current estimates of national income.

County Business Patterns

The County Business Patterns report, which originated in 1946, represents the earliest large-scale use of administrative records as a source of information that is usually available only from censuses. The report is derived from information collected for the administration of the Federal Insurance Contributions Act (Social Security). The employment and payroll data submitted quarterly by employers provide a comprehensive source of information on industrial employment levels and on the amounts of compensation on which the employers made their Social Security contribution. The reports suffer from a significant limitation, however, since contributions are made only on earnings up to a specified level, which may be exceeded by some workers as early as the first quarter of the year. This dollar level has been increased over the years with the rise in earnings, but it still complicates interpretation of the results.

The joint Social Security Administration/Census Bureau County Business Patterns report was a landmark in providing intercensal data for areas as small as counties. It constitutes the only available source of comprehensive county data on year-to-year changes in first-quarter employment and payrolls classified by industrial group. Since most workers do not earn more than the cutoff amount in a single quarter, the first quarter earnings usually reflect the full wage income.

After a period of joint publication, the Census Bureau took over full responsibility for the report but, of course, continued to depend upon data furnished by Social Security, supplemented by a special canvass of multi-unit companies.

The series was compiled on an annual basis from 1946 to 1951, at three-year intervals from 1953 to 1963, and annually since 1964. For many years, the full value of the County Business Patterns series was not realized because of the considerable delay in getting out the results. More recently, however, it has been possible to have the reports available within about a year after the end of the period to which they apply.

An improvement of considerable importance is the proposed expansion of the County Business Patterns report to cover total payrolls for the year. When this is accomplished, the county (and possibly metropolitan area) information on the distribution of total wage income within industrial groups should prove extremely useful.

One of the outstanding advantages of this series is its extremely low cost. A substantial amount of data for each county is furnished at an annual cost of a little more than $100 per area. The cost of providing similar data from a sample survey is not easy to estimate, but the economic censuses are taken at an average cost of about $7,500 per county. Economic censuses, of course, yield much more detail than the County Business Patterns reports on each establishment covered, but the reports include many kinds of businesses outside the scope of the economic censuses.

Current Population Survey

For more than twenty-five years, the main source of intercensal statistics in the field of population has been the Current Population Survey. This is undoubtedly the oldest continuing national survey of an entire country. Since it is a fairly large survey (currently about 50,000 households) and since it has always been on a monthly basis, the total expenditures for this purpose exceed those for any other single survey. It has been an important proving ground for the testing of improved techniques and has been followed closely by technical personnel in this country and abroad.

The origins of the survey were completely independent of the Census Bureau. The officials of the Research Division of the Work Projects Administration (WPA), where the survey was initiated, like many professionals in the government in the 1930's, felt the need for better information on the volume of unemployment, particularly in view of the large expenditures for unemployment relief and federal work programs. The traditional approach of deriving unemployment as the difference between projections of the total labor force and the total number employed left much to be desired.

The 1936 *Literary Digest* Presidential election poll had revealed how misleading a large sample could be if the selection method was biased, when on the basis of some 2 million returns, Roosevelt's share of the vote was underestimated by nearly 20 percentage points. On the other hand, the work of the pollsters showed that very small samples based upon properly determined quotas could yield useful and reliable estimates. John N. Webb, assistant director of the WPA Research Division, was fortunate to have two remarkably imaginative and vigorous young mathematical statisticians on his staff, Lester R. Frankel and J. Stevens Stock, who were later to acquire national reputations in sampling and survey work.

In addition, much progress was being made in developing new concepts for measuring employment and unemployment. The older concept, based upon ability and willingness to work, was found to be so subjective in character that a completely new approach was needed. The new concept was based upon the actual activity of a person, whether working, looking for work, or doing something else during the time period specified for the survey—usually a single week. The first large-scale test of the new concepts took place in the sample enumeration made in connection with the National Unemployment Census of 1937.

In 1938, Webb and his two sampling technicians decided to undertake the first direct continuing measurement of unemployment. The sample design was intended to conform strictly to probability principles, with no opportunity for the canvasser to choose one family rather than another. The rule that determined inclusion was the proximity of a family to a geographic location. In practice, the method yielded a sample that was well dispersed, even though the method was later found to be subject to a significant bias. Because of heavy internal migration, a sample based upon points rather than areas tended gradually to underweight population in rapidly growing areas and to overweight that in declining areas.

It was decided that the new operation should have a shakedown period of several months before April 1, 1940, the date of the decennial census. The comparison of the national estimates from the survey with the new census totals was intended as a demonstration of the reliability of the new sample survey.

The vindication of the new sample survey was difficult because the differences between the census and the sample survey results were substantially greater than could be explained by sampling variation. In particular, the unemployment figures from the sample were significantly above those from the census. (Later research showed that the measurement of unemployment in a census is subject to a serious bias.) But on the whole, the survey figures stood up very well under the detailed testing and comparisons undertaken by an interagency group of experts under Bureau of the Budget auspices, and the usefulness of the new approach was generally conceded.

The next question affecting the new survey, called the Monthly Report on the Labor Force (MRLF), arose in 1941, when it became apparent that the declining activity of WPA made it necessary to transfer the survey to some permanent agency. By that time, the importance of the survey was generally recognized throughout the government, and two or three agencies were much interested in receiving the function. The Bureau of Labor Statistics was a claimant because of the central importance of employment and unemployment data to the Department of Labor and because of the close relationship between the data on household employment and the employment and payroll figures that the Bureau collected from employers. The Census Bureau was convinced of the potentialities of the survey as a means of providing intercensal information on many of the subjects covered in the decennial census. The Social Security Administration also expressed interest in the survey. The decision regarding the disposition of the survey was the responsibility of the Office of Statistical Standards of the Bureau of the Budget, and extensive review and interagency discussion took place during the second and third quarters of 1942, and finally responsibility for the survey was transferred to the Bureau of the Census. At the same time, an interagency committee was set up with responsibility for continued review of the operations of the program.

In the three decades that followed, intensive work was put into strengthening the system for measuring month-to-month as well as year-to-year changes in labor force activity and for meeting the need for many measures of population change between censuses. In keeping with the broadening of the functions, the survey was renamed the Current Population Survey (CPS) in 1947. The most important features of the development of the Current Population Survey included sample design, estimation techniques, processing adaptations, and the steady broadening of the purposes served.

One continuing feature of the survey design has been the clustering of the interviews in a fixed geographical area, so that supervisory attention can ensure conformity with prescribed rules in the selection of households and in the application of the labor force concepts. Within this broad framework, however, sweeping changes have taken place. Perhaps the most important was the substitution of area sampling for the fixed-point approach. By providing for the full coverage of households within predetermined small areas, it was possible to eliminate the biases due to extremely diverse patterns of growth in different areas of the country.

The size of the monthly sample has been increased from time to time to the present level of about 50,000 households in order to hold the sampling and nonsampling components of error, as well as the total cost of the survey, to reasonable levels.

The two-stage sample plan involves the selection first of a sample of some 450 counties or combinations of counties drawn from strata set up on the basis of common economic or geographic characteristics. Then, within these counties or combinations of counties, the sampling is based on procedures that utilize lists of addresses from the latest census for about two-thirds of the country, area samples for the remainder (where addresses are not available), and samples of building permits to reflect new housing since the last census. The sample thus obtained properly reflects the changing distribution of the population and avoids the distortion that would result from the use of fixed quotas of households or persons.

It is advantageous both for accuracy and economy to interview the same households over a period of months. Experience with such panels indicates that a period of eight months is probably about as long as a family should remain in the panel. The system of rotation (four months in, eight months out, and four months in) gives good measures of month-to-month and year-to-year changes, without having an unreasonably long period of inclusion for any particular household.

Because of the potentially serious impact of response errors and biases on the statistical results, about one-third of the Current Population Survey field collection budget is devoted to various procedures to ensure and control quality. The major procedures include training, observation, reinterview, and inspection of returns. New interviewers receive extensive training during the first three months of their employment and then have additional training in the form of home study materials and periodic group training sessions. The standard program of observation requires supervisors to observe experienced interviewers about twice a year, with additional observations for those showing substandard performance. The reinterview program requires the supervisor periodically to review a subsample of households already enumerated. The results of these checks may call for additional training or for the replacement of a substandard worker. Finally, there is a review of the completed questionnaires for thoroughness and consistency, especially for the new interviewers.

Because of its various uses, the Current Population Survey has come to be regarded as a social survey yielding measures of wide usefulness as guides to U.S. public and private policy. The simplest form of utilization has been to add supplementary questions to the form, which are asked after the standard inquiries on the labor force. Under the guidance of the Office of Management and Budget, there is much interagency participation in reaching decisions concerning priorities for the additional questions to be used over a period of months. Among the significant recurring supplements are those for family income and work experience during the past year, migration, household composition, marital status, characteristics of the farm population, and school attendance. The supplements are not restricted to inquiries that have appeared in the decennial census. Questions relating to voting and registration, consumer anticipations, smoking habits, and labor union membership have also been asked.

It is safe to say that the aggregate uses of this survey have greatly exceeded the anticipations of those who participated in its origin. It has not only been an exceptional source of information on current changes, but has also proven a flexible medium for varied experimentation and progress in technological research that has benefited the government and private sectors.

FOREIGN TRADE STATISTICS

The foreign trade statistics program differs greatly from the intercensal statistics program described in the preceding section. It is basically a large-scale tabulation of statistics from official records, yielding data that have no direct relationships to any census bench marks.

The first Congress provided for the compilation of statistics of foreign trade. For the young nation, the importance of trade with other countries was apparent. Throughout U.S. history, trade information has had important uses also in connection with the revenues from import duties.

Since 1790, the Congress has given various agencies the responsibility for compiling and publishing trade statistics. When the Department of Commerce and Labor was created in 1903, it had the task of selecting and publishing annual figures on foreign trade. Another thirty-eight years elapsed, however, before responsibility for the trade statistics was shifted to the Bureau of the Census, in order to centralize the work on large-scale statistical functions—at least within the Department of Commerce.

With the continuing growth in the nation's foreign trade, the outstanding feature of the compiling task is the very large number of documents that flow into the Bureau from the 350 U.S. ports. The total number in an average month is about 800,000, two-thirds of them for exports and the remainder for imports. The documents serve for the administration of customs or export control and for preparation of statistics on import and export trade. The dual nature of the documents to some extent reduces their acceptability for statistical purposes, since the information may be tailored to fit customs or export control regulations. The review of the documents by customs officials is, of course, intended to ensure that they are adequate for statistical purposes. In addition, an educational program has been directed at the largest shippers to familiarize them with the rules for the proper preparation of documents for statistical purposes.

Commodity and Country Detail

Information about the amount and value of shipments into and out of the country is of limited value to many users unless it is organized according to commodity and country. The commodity information is shown for about 4,000 export and 2,400 import commodity categories. Country detail is shown for approximately 150 countries, and Customs District detail for about 50 such districts.

Because of the variety of purposes served by foreign trade statistics, the subject of commodity classification is of great importance. The basic monthly statistics are published in terms of Schedule B, "Statistical Classification of Domestic and Foreign Commodities Exported from the United States," for exports, and in terms of Schedule A, "Statistical Classification of Commodities Imported into the United States," for imports. Schedule A and Schedule B are based on the United Nations Standard International Trade Classification (Revised), used by most nations of the world. For imports, commodity classification is also furnished in terms of the roughly 10,000 commodity classifications of the Tariff Schedules of the United States (Annotated). Furthermore, both import and export data are presented annually in terms of some 2,000 commodity classifications based upon the United States Standard Industrial Classification so that exports and imports can be related to the nation's industrial output. No standard classification is ever fully abreast of the technical developments that bring new products into the field of foreign trade, and hence there are many requests for expansion of the list.

The large monthly volume of trade documents would seem to make foreign trade statistics an unusually good candidate for sampling. However, the large number of commodities and countries by which the documents are classified leads to a very low frequency in many of the tabulation cells. With any significant use of sampling, the errors for many of the cells would be relatively high. Accordingly, the chief means of reducing processing costs has been to introduce differential treatment for the smaller items. In view of the large number of fairly small transactions, it is possible to make significant savings by eliminating those below a certain cutoff level or by processing only a part of those in a low-volume range. Even this modest attempt at cost reduction through sampling and cutoffs has caused protests, since some foreign trade observers are interested in the international movement of small quantities of certain commodities that show new trade patterns.

Imports, Exports, and Shipping

The most widely used foreign trade statistics show the monthly imports and exports classified by commodity and by country. Thanks to the extensive use of computers, these are available in a number of forms. For those wishing information on a considerable segment of foreign trade, the large monthly summary publications are likely to prove most useful. Some of the more detailed tables are not available in conventional published form, but can be obtained in the form of computer tapes, microfilm, or hard copy reproduced from microfilm. In order to facilitate use of the basic trade statistics, many derived figures useful for analysis are included, such as cumulative totals and seasonally adjusted figures for many of the monthly series.

Although the basic and special reports that have been described take care of most of the needs of other government agencies, there are a few cases when special arrangements may appear to overlap the work of the Census Bureau. Actually, however, there is little true duplication.

For example, the Bureau of Customs publishes import statistics on commodities that are under import quota, showing the established quota and the amount that has been filled as of a given date. These reports are usually discontinued after the quota for a given calendar year has been filled.

The Department of Agriculture issues reports on imports of cheese and other dairy products against licenses that relate to certain import quotas in force under the Agricultural Adjustment Act. The Oil Import Administration of the Department of the Interior issues monthly news releases on imports of crude oil and oil products showing imports licensed under the mandatory oil import program, as well as imports of items exempt from the program. Most of the data are completely different from those published by the Census Bureau, since they are classified in terms of barrels per day imported by name of importer. The Bureau of Mines issues another report presenting some important statistics on crude petroleum, petroleum products, and natural-gas-liquids. In the main, the data are derived from the information on imports that is furnished by petroleum companies in their monthly refinery report to the Bureau of Mines. A quite different kind of report is the information on foreign cargoes entered at leading U.S. ports, which is published in a weekly *Import Bulletin* by the Journal of Commerce. These data are obtained from Bureau of Customs vessel manifest forms and include quantity information but no values.

These reports by agencies operating regulatory or control programs serve highly specialized needs that probably could not be met equally well by additional work on the part of the Census Bureau, which is clearly the only comprehensive source of information on the nation's trade with other countries.

For users of foreign trade statistics primarily interested in the method of transportation rather than quantity and value of commodities, tabulations are prepared in terms of shipping weight as well as value, subdivided according to the method of transportation. The Maritime Administration, the Army Corps of Engineers, and the Civil Aeronautics Board, as well as companies engaged in shipping goods, are major users of statistics on methods of transportation.

Because of the wide variety of purposes served by foreign trade statistics, they are rearranged and put into a number of special packages. For example, vessel and shipping data are shown for about 150 U.S. ports of lading and unlading and for about 1,500 foreign ports. Because of widespread interest in the effect of tariff policies, data are made available for each of 10,000 tariff schedules with additional information for calculated import duties collected. Special tabulations are also prepared for use in the determination of quotas, as back-up for trade negotiations, or for determining assistance to be given through grants-in-aid. Through special work on the trade documents, it is often possible to provide data on a particular commodity, even though it is not recognized in the standard classification. Through such special work, quite specific needs of the government or of a business firm can sometimes be met on an individual basis.

A number of useful series of current statistics have been omitted from the above account—not because they are unimportant, but because they do not contribute anything new with respect to the origins or technical development of current statistics. Among these are current reports on cotton-ginning and production, construction, housing, wholesale trade, services, state and local government finances and employment, and air-borne and water-borne commerce.

VI

The Bureau as a Statistical Service Agency

From the vantage point of the present, it is easy to see why the Census Bureau has become the general-purpose statistical agency of the federal government. It is much less apparent why the Bureau had so little continuing service work until the early 1950's (see Table III, Chapter II). At first, there was, of course, little opportunity to undertake service work for other agencies. The task of tooling up for each census was so heavy that there was little chance to do such outside work unless it was directly tied to the current census. Furthermore, the temporary nature of the census organization made it almost impossible for the Superintendent of the Census to enter into any service contracts.

The establishment of the permanent bureau in 1902 removed one barrier to the undertaking of service work, but the Act referred only to special tabulations based upon the census and thus gave no encouragement to other service work.

The first significant account of work performed by the Census Bureau was a 1909 statement by Director Simon N. D. North, referring to work done for the Secretary of the Treasury in tabulating data for the state, county, and municipal bonds available for use under the new Currency Act. He mentioned also work in progress for the National Conservation Commission and the Commission on the Improvement of Country Life. All of these functions were purely clerical in character, in accordance with the Director's thought that the Bureau's force of trained clerks could be applied to an emergency undertaking, assuring speed, economy, and accuracy.

During World War I, the Census Director offered the services of up to one hundred clerks for periods as long as six months to meet the wartime needs of other agencies for such tasks as addressing envelopes, making tabulations for the Shipping Board, classifying the occupations of draft registrants, and performing miscellaneous operations for the American Red Cross, the Justice Department, and other agencies. In the 1930's, the Census Bureau assisted the Federal Emergency Relief Administration and made tabulations of the personnel and work performance of the Civilian Conservation Corps.

More closely related to the Bureau's mission were special censuses of local areas and additional tabulations of the material collected in the periodic censuses. The first special census was taken in Tulsa, Oklahoma, in 1915. This was followed by a succession of similar jobs for cities needing information on population changes since the latest decennial census. During World War I, a number of jobs done for other agencies involved either special tabulations of the schedules collected in the most recent census or required the collection of new information. For example, a special survey was made of commercial greenhouses in order to determine their fuel requirements. In the early 1940's, when the Bureau's program of current industrial statistics was still quite fragmentary, the War Production Board engaged the Census Bureau in very substantial collection operations necessary to supply the up-to-date information called for by its wartime responsibilities.

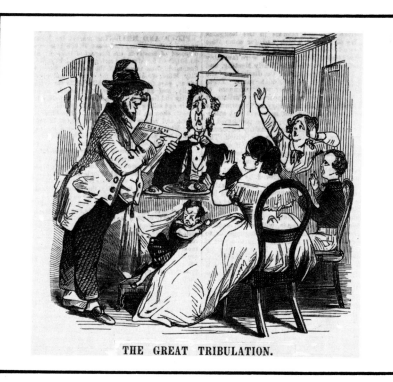

THE GREAT TRIBULATION.

This cartoon from an 1860 *Saturday Evening Post* illustrates the hair-tearing that accompanied the taking of the census of 1860. The caption reads: "CENSUS MARSHAL.—'I jist want to know how many of yez is deaf, dumb, blind, insane and idiotic—likewise how many convicts there is in the family .—what all your ages are, especially the old woman and the young ladies— and how many dollars the old gentleman is worth.'"

The 1870 census was a more placid affair, according to this century-old engraving from *Harper's Weekly* of November 19, 1870.

An inquisitive census-taker of 1890 puzzles a family on New York's East Side in this cover cartoon from Frank Leslie's popular weekly. The numbered questions at the bottom of the page apply to the characters in the squares:

QUESTION 19—"Are you able to read?" QUESTION 21—"Able to speak English?" QUESTION 23—"Are you defective in mind, sight, hearing, or speech, or crippled, maimed, or deformed? State name of defect." QUESTION 24—"Are you a prisoner, convict, homeless child, or pauper?"

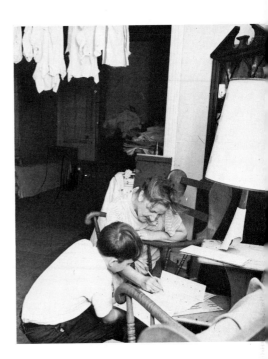

A 1970 census enumerator gains the confidence of a senior citizen *(above left)*. A low-income family fills out its own census-by-mail form *(above right)*. Although each person approached by the census-taker is required by law to answer the questions asked, he knows that his replies are confidential. The Census Bureau's policy of confidentiality is stated in the poster below.

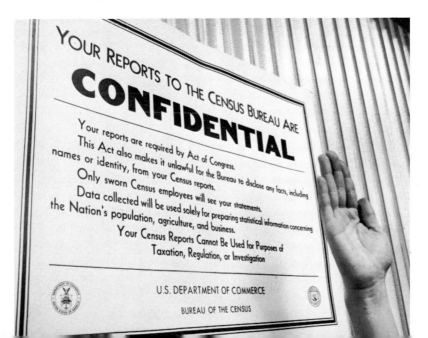

YOUR REPORTS TO THE CENSUS BUREAU ARE

CONFIDENTIAL

Your reports are required by Act of Congress.
This Act also makes it unlawful for the Bureau to disclose any facts, including names or identity, from your Census reports.
Only sworn Census employees will see your statements.
Data collected will be used solely for preparing statistical information concerning the Nation's population, agriculture, and business.
Your Census Reports Cannot Be Used for Purposes of Taxation, Regulation, or Investigation

U.S. DEPARTMENT OF COMMERCE

BUREAU OF THE CENSUS

CENSUS TOOLS—The Punched Card Era

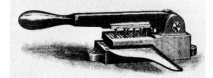

Above: The "gang punch" was an important element of the system. The Hollerith system was used in tabulating the censuses of 1890 and 1900.

Left: The first complete, electrical census-tabulating system was developed by Herman Hollerith in the 1880's.

The 1890 pantograph punch was used, with improvements, through the 1920 census.

Automatic tabulating machines of the 1920's like this one were used as recently as 1950.

This automatic sorter was built by the Census Bureau in 1918.

CENSUS TOOLS — The Computer Era

The 1951 UNIVAC I computer system in operation: Its speeds were modest in terms of later equipment but far in advance of those achieved by the punched card system.

FOSDIC (Film Optical Sensing Device for Input to Computers): FOSDIC-prepared input saved seven months and more than $5 million in tabulating the 1960 census. Savings in the 1970 census were approximately $10 million.

This Map Area Computer is currently in use by the Bureau of the Census.

The 1920 census was tabulated here in the old "Tempo C" building in Washington, D.C., half a century ago. Today, the Bureau maintains two sizable field installations in addition to its facilities at Suitland, Maryland.

A wide range of Census Bureau programs are processed at the Jeffersonville, Indiana, Data Preparation Division. Its processing facilities at the peak of 1970 census-processing included the forty microfilm cameras shown here.

The Personal Census Service Branch at Pittsburg, Kansas, can provide personal census-record information—on a fee basis—for every individual recorded in the decennial censuses.

Census-built
high-speed
microfilming
equipment
photographs 1970
census forms
at the rate of
two per second.

Composite
census maps
are assembled
from various
sources in the
Census Bureau
installation at
Jeffersonville,
Indiana.

A map of
metropolitan
Saint Louis
is prepared
for purposes
of census
enumeration.

President Lyndon Johnson is present in the Department of Commerce Building on November 20, 1967, as the census clock strikes 200,000,000. (In 1943, a Census Bureau booklet contained this statement: "Authorities estimate that by about 1980 our population growth will have stopped altogether at a peak of around 153 millions." Present Bureau projections for 1980 range from 228,000,000 to 234,000,000!)

Tulo Montenegro, now Secretary General of the Inter-American Statistical Institute, receives his training certificate from Assistant Director Eckler *(left)* on August 20, 1948.

The Order of the White Elephant— an award given to a Census Bureau adviser in Thailand in 1965.

Although these types of service functions have continued to play an important role in the Bureau's program, they account for only a small part of the Bureau's explosive growth in the 1950's and 1960's. That expansion represented in large part the utilization by many agencies of the broad survey capability that was developed in the Census Bureau during the 1940's, when it was necessary for the Bureau to acquire the human and material resources required for modern survey operations. The almost exclusively clerical organization of the early 1930's now included mathematical statisticians and professionals who were specialists in subject fields and survey operations. The Bureau's extensive files and maps were of great importance in providing efficient samples of population and establishments. Experience was developed in schedule design, in the wording of questionnaires, the preparation of instructions for the field organization, and the planning of tabulations and publications. A staff experienced in field supervision and an interviewing staff were also prerequisites. Less attention was initially required in connection with tabulating equipment, since the Bureau's facilities for carrying out complete censuses were more than adequate for tabulating sample-based data. Even here, the development of the multi-column sorter for the 1950 census and the introduction of the first electronic data processing equipment early in the 1950's provided an important base for the greatly expanded service functions that were to follow.

The earliest significant example of the survey operation type of service work was the National Unemployment Census of 1937, which was undertaken long before the completion of the professional and technological developments mentioned above. In connection with this census, the Bureau was called upon to set up a sample survey to supplement and check the results of the post card registration. In designing the questionnaire, setting up the sample design, and arranging for the collection of the information by means of the postal carriers, the Bureau introduced important advances in the field of labor force surveys.

LEGISLATIVE AND ADMINISTRATIVE DEVELOPMENTS

Both before and after the National Unemployment Census of 1937, there were a number of administrative and legislative developments that combined to pave the way for a sharp rise in the Bureau's service operations. Initially, however, the 1937 report of the Committee on Government Statistics and Information Services seemed a barrier to the kind of change that was to come later. It affirmed the principle that statistical work should be divided among federal agencies on the basis of the focal interests of the agencies. Fortunately, Stuart Rice, who as assistant director of the Bureau of the Budget was in charge of coordinating federal statistics for two decades, perceived the dangers of dispersing statistical efforts too widely. His office, under the provisions of the Federal Reports Act, was influential in the distribution of statistical work among agencies, both by influencing the allocation of new functions and by altering the arrangements for existing functions.

Perhaps the most important evidence of the interest of the Budget Bureau was their decision regarding the Monthly Report on the Labor Force of the Works Projects Administration (WPA), described in the preceding chapter. The best indication of the Budget Bureau's interest in the service function is the following excerpt from Rice's letter to the Census Director:

> Because of the wide utilization of the Section's facilities by other agencies which is in prospect and because of the experimental character of its work and our interest in it as a servicing unit for the Federal Government generally it is understood that the Bureau of the Budget will appoint an advisory committee

to assist the Section in bringing its facilities to the attention of other Federal agencies and in reaching technical decisions upon the various opportunities for service which are presented to it.

The transfer of this survey to the Bureau of the Census in 1942 added significantly to the Bureau's general survey capabilities by providing a field organization and a national population panel, which had already been frequently used for service work.

Through the 1940's and 1950's this survey, renamed the Current Population Survey (CPS) in 1947, was sufficient to meet most of the immediate needs of federal agencies, generally through the addition of supplementary questions. By 1962, however, demands for data derived from surveys had exceeded the capacity of the CPS, and the Bureau developed a new national operation called the Quarterly Household Survey (QHS). A part of the Bureau's own program of current statistics, as well as some of the reimbursable work, have been carried out by the QHS.

Earlier, however, after the transfer of the WPA survey, the needs of World War II agencies for statistical information became more extensive. This time there was a sharp break from World War I practice. The coordinating influence of the Budget Bureau led to much greater use of the facilities of existing agencies in lieu of setting up new collection functions. The assignments given to the Census Bureau included a series of consumer requirement surveys for the War Production Board to measure shortages in household items, durable goods, clothing, services, and repairs. A somewhat similar survey pertained to farm supplies and equipment. For the Office of Price Administration, the Census Bureau collected information by means of a so-called Wartime Food Diary, which provided fast weekly reports from civilians on food purchasing under point-rationing. The consumer panel used for the Wartime Food Diary also yielded information on the number of unused points for meat and processed foods, for sugar, and other special items, as well as information on shoe-ration stamps and the inventories of shoes. Surveys of housing for the National Housing Agency measured the current housing supply in areas of war activity and revealed the need for new construction. In the field of economic statistics, the industrial information compiled for the War Production Board was later to provide the basis for a greatly strengthened program of current information.

After World War II, a number of administrative and legal developments laid a solid basis for the expansion of service activities to be performed by the Census Bureau. For example, the report of the 1947 Hoover Commission (whose work has been referred to in Chapter II) gave considerable attention to the organization of statistical work in the federal government and concluded that repetitive and large-scale tasks should generally be concentrated in a single agency. The Budget and Accounting Procedures Act of 1950 gave an explicit basis for organizing the statistical work of the entire government. One of the objectives mentioned in this Act was "to achieve the most effective use of resources available for statistical work by the agencies, in relation to over-all needs." It thus provided a more specific statistical support for the Economy Act of 1932. Clearly, these developments permitted the allocation of statistical work for the most effective use of the available resources.

As a direct result of these technological, administrative, and legislative developments in the 1940's and 1950's, the Bureau's service functions have grown much more rapidly than the census and survey programs paid out of appropriations made directly to the Bureau and also more rapidly than the rest of the statistical work of the government. Most of the expansion has taken place in the field of statistical survey operation, including both professional and clerical functions.

None of this expansion would have taken place, of course, unless there had been a need for the data. For this, credit must go to the new social consciousness of the 1960's. As a consequence of the government programs instituted during these years in the fields of the alleviation of poverty, federal aid to education, medical care insurance for the elderly—to mention only a few—the demand for program-oriented data to aid in planning, appraising, and evaluating grew rapidly. Having proven itself able and willing to provide these special services, and having demonstrated beyond question the utility of the results, the Bureau needed only to determine how far it should go in meeting the total demand for such work.

It is not universally realized that expansion of the Bureau's service function means receiving some of the advantages of a centralized statistical system while adhering to the focal agency concept. An example of the relationship between the two approaches was provided by the action of the Budget Bureau in 1959, when it transferred to the Bureau of Labor Statistics responsibility for planning, analysis, and publication of the labor force segment of the Current Population Survey. Since the initial transfer from WPA in 1942, the Census Bureau had regularly published the employment and unemployment figures from the quarterly household survey, while the Bureau of Labor Statistics collected and published the statistics on establishment employment and payrolls. During that period, the Census Bureau was carrying out in this field a role similar to that of a central bureau of statistics, such as the Dominion Bureau of Statistics of Canada (now known as Statistics Canada). In that country, the results of the labor force survey have always been published by the Dominion Bureau, but the Ministry of Labor, which is responsible for the government's labor policies, makes further use of the materials, whether published or unpublished. In this country, however, under the focal agency principle, the Bureau of Labor Statistics was able to make a strong case for greater control of the labor force data, so that the Bureau of the Budget approved the shift. The immediate result, in terms of appropriations, was to reduce the amounts requested annually by the Census Bureau for the conduct of the current statistics program. At the same time, funds appropriated to the Bureau of Labor Statistics were correspondingly increased, and that Bureau transferred the increase to the Bureau of the Census by means of an annual service contract. The retention by Census of the responsibility for the survey functions, such as design, sample selection, quality control, collection, processing, and tabulating work, made possible the continuation of the technical gains resulting from coordinating the management of large-scale statistical activities. Before the transfer as well as after, the agencies have continuously been in close contact through the use of an interagency committee. Hence, the change in sponsorship has involved no great change in methods of operation.

Surveys for Other Agencies

The surveys undertaken for other agencies have varied so much in purpose, scope, and methodology that comprehensive coverage is impracticable. Some of the more interesting examples are those that have been carried out in the fields of housing, health, welfare, and social security.*

Housing

The various housing agencies have been responsible for the largest number of surveys over the longest period. Since housing markets vary greatly from city to city, the pattern in this field has been to set up a series of local surveys to measure the degree of overcrowding or, alternatively, to show the seriousness of the vacancy problem in different cities. During

* One important additional example of service operations is the field work for the Consumer Expenditures Survey, needed by the Bureau of Labor Statistics for the decennial updating of the Consumer Price Index. Most of the work other than testing will be done in 1972 and later. The allocation of this work to the Census Bureau is in line with the principles set forth in the original report of the 1947 Hoover Commission.

World War II, such surveys were used in connection with the measurement of existing housing supply in areas of war activity and in estimating the need for new construction of both public and private war housing. Later, similar inquiries were used by local housing authorities as a basis for determining public housing requirements. In the last few years, this type of survey has been continued only in New York City, where the rent control provisions call for periodic information on the vacancy situation. Other inquiries have been undertaken for the U.S. Department of Housing and Urban Development to determine methods of financing large-scale properties, characteristics of newly constructed housing units, and the rate at which new apartments are being absorbed into the housing market. Through these undertakings, the sponsoring agency gains information on the relationship between housing costs and family resources, ascertaining the extent to which residential building activity is meeting the needs of various segments of the population.

Health

The initiation of the national health survey in 1957 marked the beginning of one of the most noteworthy service contracts undertaken by the Census Bureau. This survey is designed to give a continuing flow of information on the volume and character of illness and disability, the medical care received, utilization of health facilities, and related demographic, social, and economic variables. The survey has demonstrated the feasibility of combined use of the professional competence of the health statisticians in the National Center for Health Statistics (NCHS) and of the mathematical and survey statisticians of the Bureau of the Census. The possibility of this kind of joint operation had previously been tested by work carried out in California under the sponsorship of the state's public health agency. At the federal level, the NCHS and Census Bureau personnel collaborated closely in the design of the survey operation, the content of the questionnaire and instructions, the processing, and the tabulation plans. Since the interviewing was to be carried out on a continuing basis throughout the year, a special interviewing staff was created to take care of the national health survey program. All work connected with the preparation of reports and the analysis of the results was the responsibility of the NCHS. Thus, the survey demonstrated the feasibility of an arrangement that took into account the focal interest of NCHS in public health matters and, at the same time, benefited from the increased efficiency resulting from the coordination of this survey with other large-scale statistical undertakings.

From a modest beginning the data needs of the health community have expanded until now the Bureau conducts a considerable number of related projects, such as the hospital discharge survey, which provides information on diagnoses and charges collected from medical records in a sample of general hospitals, and surveys of nursing homes, homes for the aged, and similar facilities. Surveys also are conducted for the purpose of identifying specific subgroups of the population who are subsequently asked to participate in a health examination conducted by doctors on the staff of the Public Health Service.

Welfare and Public Assistance

A considerable number of surveys have been designed to furnish information on some segment of the population likely to require assistance from public sources. The most extensive survey operations in this area were the surveys of economic opportunity in 1966 and 1967, conducted for the Office of Economic Opportunity. These measured certain economic and demographic characteristics and income sources of families and individuals throughout the country, particularly those living in the sections classified as poverty areas. In general, the samples for these inquiries were not large enough to provide information for particular locations. One notable exception was the so-called Watts survey, conducted shortly after the rioting in Los Angeles in order to learn about employment, housing, income, and other characteristics of the population living near the site of the riots. Other surveys have been aimed at a particular population class; the survey of senior citizens in 1963 and the survey of disabled adults in 1966 were both designed to provide a basis for improving programs for their respective groups.

Other Surveys

The Social Security Administration (SSA) and the Manpower Administration have called upon the Census Bureau to interview a panel of individuals over a period of years to determine changes in their status. At the request of the Social Security Administration, a sample of persons between 50 and 63 years of age was selected and will be followed up every 2 years over a 10-year period to obtain information on problems and adjustments incidental to retirement and to withdrawal from the labor force. In a separate undertaking, the Manpower Administration has sponsored a series of four surveys which the Bureau of the Census is conducting. Information has been collected from samples of young women and young men from 14 to 24 years of age, and of women 30 to 44 years of age and of men 45 to 59 years old. The economic and demographic information collected has revealed facts regarding introduction into the labor force, has provided insight into the choice of pursuits, and for the older workers has led to an understanding of the employment problems they encounter. These highly sophisticated surveys are landmarks in the development of dynamic measures of the economic progress of individual workers.

Examples of surveys conducted since 1960 by the Bureau of the Census for other federal agencies will be found in Table VII. None of these is discussed elsewhere in this chap-

TABLE VII

EXAMPLES OF SURVEYS CONDUCTED BY THE BUREAU OF THE CENSUS
FOR OTHER FEDERAL AGENCIES SINCE 1960

Detailed Survey of the Unemployed: 1962–63 (Department of Labor) —to provide additional insight into the problems of unemployment.

Survey of Draft Age Men: 1964 (Department of Defense)—to provide information to assist in the review of the draft system and defense manpower needs.

National Survey of Volunteer Work: 1965 (Department of Labor)— a first attempt to quantify the extent of volunteer, unpaid work, by type.

Urban Employment Survey: 1968 to date (Department of Labor)— to explore the employment problems over time of those living in ghetto areas in a limited number of large urban centers.

British-Norwegian Health Survey: 1963 (National Heart Institute/National Cancer Institute)—to determine the health characteristics of migrants from the United Kingdom and Norway as one step in an international study comparing migrants and native-born populations.

Current Medicare Survey: 1966 to date (Social Security Administration)—to provide current measures of the extent and costs of use of medical facilities by those registered for phase "B" of Medicare.

National Recreation Survey: 1960–61 (Outdoor Recreation Resources Review Commission)—a series of national surveys to develop information on the recreation habits and preferences of the population, to assist in developing national goals in this area.

Survey of the Economic and Social Effects of Traffic Accident Injuries: 1969 (Department of Transportation)—A national survey of persons injured in traffic accidents, conducted at the request of the Congress, as one phase of an over-all review of the current automobile insurance system.

---

ter. (Work performed by the Bureau for the Law Enforcement Assistance Administration of the Justice Department will be described in Chapter X.)

Special Censuses; Other Classes of Service Work

The work load due to special censuses is a highly variable one, reaching its low in the first year or two after a decennial census and rising to peak levels in the years when the census is most seriously out of date. The load also varies markedly from state to state because of differences in growth rates and in the laws governing the distribution of public funds. For a number of years, special censuses were extremely numerous in California, where population growth has been very rapid and where the increase in receipts from the gasoline tax might be more than enough to pay for the cost of censuses taken once a year or more often. Recently, funds have been distributed on the basis of estimates for all communities as prepared by a state commission, and there is no longer any incentive for taking special censuses. In New York State, the amendment of the State Finance Law and the General Municipal Law in 1956 enabled communities to qualify for a higher amount of state funds through special censuses taken as of April 1, in any year. Under the terms of this legislation, the Census Bureau has been requested to take a number of special censuses each spring in those communities with a growth expected to be sufficient to make this action profitable. During the 1960's, the Bureau took censuses of over 1,600 communities including states, counties, cities, and villages.

A number of the service functions carried out by the Census Bureau are not at all related to the collection, processing, and tabulation of data.

The search for individual census records, which dates back fifty years, has provided a direct service to about 8 million individuals who lack other means of proving age, citizenship, or other facts about themselves. Such work was particularly heavy during World War II and at the time of the introduction of Medicare.

Under the State Department's foreign assistance program, the Bureau has rendered a special service in the training of foreign nationals and the provision of advisers to aid foreign governments in their statistical development. These activities will be described in Chapter XIII. Another type of service performed for the State Department is the development of a sophisticated data system for assessing population problems and evaluating family planning programs in developing countries. This system helps the State Department evaluate the benefits derived from its assistance programs and determine how they should be changed.

GUIDELINES FOR SERVICE WORK

Much attention has been given to the development of guidelines for conducting surveys for other organizations. These principles have gradually evolved as a result of the collaborative efforts of the Office of Management and Budget and the Bureau. Assistance in the formulation of these principles and in the evaluation of the Bureau's plans for new kinds of service work has been provided by the Census Advisory Committee appointed by the President of the American Statistical Association.

In the Bureau's early years, service work was regarded as a way of facilitating the retention of trained clerks. During World War II, however it became apparent that a service agency would be of only partial utility to other agencies, if its services were assured solely when the agency's own work load was light. Since then progress has been made in the establishment of flexible arrangements permitting the assumption of additional tasks on comparatively short notice. The ability to hire additional staff on a temporary basis is an important element, but equally important to the Bureau is the willingness of the staff to make all-out efforts in response to the needs of another agency.

Much consideration is given to the suitability of projects that the Census Bureau is asked to undertake. Without exception, a project must serve the public interest, if it is to be done by the Bureau. Some of the work proposed by other agencies is turned down because of the adverse effect it might have on the Bureau's recurring inquiries. For example, a survey might not be accepted because of the exceptionally heavy load imposed upon respondents. Likewise, questions relating to religious preference have been excluded because the controversy arising from the service contract might later have an adverse effect upon the Current Population Survey or the decennial census. The battery of inquiries sometimes used to measure degree of alienation has also been excluded because they can readily be taken out of context and made to seem completely trivial in nature. Other subjects which have been avoided are alcoholism, use of drugs, and identification of commercial brands.

The Bureau's policy is to limit its data collection activities to those undertakings that will give results conforming to a reasonable standard of accuracy. In some cases, the questions proposed by the sponsor are judged not likely to provide dependable information on the basis of preliminary tests or experience of other agencies. Measurements of the number of gamblers, or the number of deaf people, or of those suffering partial blindness are subject to so large an error that the Bureau would seek to avoid such queries. In other problematic situations, the sponsor may wish to have the data tabulated in such detail that most of the figures would have very high sampling errors and the results would prove misleading or perhaps worse than useless.

The official guidelines for determining work the government should do for itself and work that should be contracted to private industry do not provide for all of the considerations that arise in statistical undertakings. In this area, the decision to have the work done by a government agency may turn upon the need to have guaranteed continuity of output, to have standards of performance a matter of public record, or have the assurance that all the data collected will be in public domain. When the Census Bureau is requested to perform work for another government agency, the principal responsibility for the decision not to contract with a private agency lies with the sponsor. Even so, the Bureau may decline to undertake a particular survey, if the sponsor's current relationship with a private organization (including the making or offering of a similar contract) indicates that the survey task could be appropriately performed outside of the government.

In summary, the use of the guidelines for service work call for the exercise of much judgment, since the necessary decisions often involve a choice between two quite evenly balanced alternatives.

VII

Research and Development

In the early 1930's, Stuart A. Rice, who was a sociologist and social scientist before he became assistant director of the Bureau of the Budget, perceived the need for a research capability in the Bureau of the Census. He specifically recommended "that the development of *research functions within the Bureau* be encouraged, without diminution of its basic fact-collecting responsibilities."

It is certain that not even Rice envisioned the potentialities for contributions from research and development to the broad field of statistical production. The expansion of aggressive marketing programs on the part of business and the increase in the number of federal agencies with large program responsibilities created demands for new types of statistical information. In addition, new techniques were required to meet the demands being made upon the periodic censuses without increasing the burden upon the respondent and without stretching the Bureau's budget beyond reasonable limits. The pressure placed upon resources for statistical work was especially great during the Depression and the war years, when dependence on statistical facts for all kinds of decisions led to a growing concern about the completeness and reliability of censuses and surveys.

Sampling

As the pressures for more detailed and more frequent statistical data mounted, the possibility was considered that sample surveys might supply estimates trustworthy enough for decision-making purposes. In the 1930's, however, sampling was more an art than a science, as the ill-fated *Literary Digest* Presidential election poll of 1936 testified. The role of the mathematical theory of probability in sample survey design was just beginning to be explored; J. Neyman's classic paper arguing for random sampling rather than purposive selection appeared in the *Journal of the Royal Statistical Society* in 1934, and the work of R. A. Fisher on the fundamental importance of randomization in experimental design was already attracting the attention of statisticians.

The assignment given the Bureau of the Census in 1937 to develop an enumerative check census of unemployment to determine what proportion of the unemployed had registered in the unemployment census is sometimes referred to as the beginning of evaluation surveys by the Bureau, but its main significance was that of a sample survey designed to measure the amount of unemployment in the entire United States. The use of postmen as canvassers in two out of every hundred postal routes gave more reliable results than a supposedly complete registration. It is likely that this procedure helped change the attitudes of officials who had long been dedicated to the principle of complete counts of the population and establishments.

Another break-through was the introduction of sampling in the 1940 census. For a designated 5 per cent of the population, information was obtained on a number of items supplementary to the main set of census inquiries. The first inquiry on income later proved to be a vital part of the census program, serving many government and business needs.

A third important development was the transfer in 1942 of

the Works Projects Administration's survey of unemployment —the Monthly Report on the Labor Force, already mentioned as a source of intercensal statistics. The Bureau thus acquired a continuing sample of the population, based upon a sample design more complex than any yet undertaken. In the years that followed, advances were made in the theory and practice of survey sample design that brought national and international recognition to the Census Bureau staff.*

One of the guiding principles followed by the research staff is that all of the Bureau's statistics based upon a sample should be so designed that the amount of error can be measured and reported to the users of the data. The second principle—the maximizing of the output per dollar of cost—operating within the framework of the first, provides a means for choice among designs. In the Bureau's efforts to balance cost against the amount of sampling error, a large volume of em-

---

* As a long-time census worker, the author cannot resist the temptation to identify, with pride, some of the individuals whose work on the research and development program mentioned in this chapter goes back to the 1940's and who have been responsible for much of the great advance made since then. First on any list would be the names of Morris H. Hansen and William N. Hurwitz. In the minds of most statisticians, these two names are coupled for their break-throughs in sampling and response research, for their joint authorship of a major text book and research papers, and for stimulation given to the remarkable staff associated with them. Among the outstanding members in the early years were William G. Madow, also a joint author of a two-volume statistical text, W. Edwards Deming, Lester R. Frankel, Joseph Steinberg, Benjamin Tepping, Harold Nisselson, Joseph Waksberg, Joseph Daly, and Max Bershad. Many of the problems which this group tackled were undertaken on a team basis, with overtime work often continuing through the late evening and early morning hours in each other's home.

Their complete absorption in their work is illustrated by a story often told by members of the car pool in which Hansen was a member. One evening, Hansen and Hurwitz were occupying the front seat and, as usual, were discussing a statistical problem with great fervor and concentration. Suddenly, at a traffic light in downtown Washington, one of them reminded the other, "this is where we need to get off." Their simultaneous departure through the two front doors left the occupants remaining in the rear nonplussed, but with an unforgettable story regarding the preoccupation of mathematical statisticians. Many people might dismiss this story as apocryphal, but having heard it confirmed by different members of the car pool, I am prepared to accept its validity.

pirical data was accumulated on the cost structure of the typical survey process and on the various parameters of the population that affect the sampling variability associated with different designs.

Sampling in Censuses

Because of the size of all operations connected with the censuses, they offered especially attractive opportunities for sampling. The following discussion applies to the population and housing censuses, where sampling has been used the most. As far as respondents are concerned, the chief use of sampling has been in the collection of data. This kind of application has been used increasingly since 1940. In 1960 and 1970, only six population questions were asked for each individual, but the number of housing questions asked of all households was about four times as great, in order to provide the battery of data published for individual city blocks. (Block statistics, if based upon a sample, would be subject to such high sampling errors as to be unacceptable to many users.)

The sharp increase in the use of sampling in the decennial censuses encountered some opposition from census users. Those with a blind faith in the accuracy of the complete counts furnished by the censuses were naturally concerned about the substitution of data subject to sampling error. The way for the fullest utilization of the sampling approach was not really open until research revealed that nonsampling errors may often be larger than sampling errors. This finding led to the realization that the over-all accuracy of a census would be improved by taking the savings due to sampling and using them to reduce the errors of response.

Important technical problems were encountered in broadening sampling in the censuses. It was found desirable to use designated lines on the census questionnaires (on which household members were successively listed) as sampling units. With this approach, it was necessary to designate the lines in such a way as to avoid bias due to the location of households on the block and the order of listing persons within a household. Other problems requiring much research were the choice between using the individual or the family as the sampling unit, and the control of enumerator routing, so as to deprive the enumerator of the ability to choose sampling units on the basis of personal convenience or acquaintance.

Another use of sampling in censuses is to provide certain tabulations more rapidly or more economically. This may take the form of advance tabulation of a sample for early evidence of changes since the preceding census. Alternatively, sampling may be used to carry out certain types of tabulations particularly valuable for analytical purposes, such as family statistics, interrelationships of detailed occupational and industrial classifications, and other complex tabulations of economic and social variables.

A third major use of sampling in connection with censuses is for control of quality in such activities as printing and assembly of schedules, collating of field materials, microfilming, coding schedules, and enumeration. The earliest application was the limitation of verification of editing and coding to a small proportion of the returns. The sampling plan was designed to provide a periodic measure of the quality of work of each individual, because the differences among individuals account for most of the variation in quality of output. A more difficult task was the application of quality control methods to the work of enumerators, because of the short time period involved, the wide dispersion of these workers, and the relatively infrequent contacts with their first line supervisors. In the 1960 and 1970 censuses, some real progress was achieved in assuring that enumerators follow instructions in conducting their interviews and in selecting sample units. The work of the enumerator was inspected by his supervisor as the work proceeded, so that problems could be dealt with as they were encountered.

Sampling in Surveys

The theory of sampling from a census is relatively simple, since the census itself provides a natural sampling frame. On the other hand, the application of sampling to statistical surveys of population, dwelling units, and establishments has involved many challenges not met in the application to censuses. In the 1940's and 1950's, much effort was put into learning how to develop and use sampling frames and sampling units that do not depend on the availability of census lists and how to design surveys to maximize the results per dollar of expenditure.

In the early days of sampling applications, the principles involved were not always easy to communicate to nontechnical people, such as members of Congress. Congressional questions were especially likely to arise at a time when the election polls had failed to indicate the actual outcome of a particular race. James C. Capt, Director of the Census from 1941 to 1949, once explained sampling to a Southern congressman who had misgivings about the validity of the new approach. Capt used the analogy of the farmer digging a hill of potatoes here and there to see how his crop was coming along. He even introduced the principle of stratification by pointing out that the farmer might take a few hills each from the bottom land and from the hilly areas of his field. He was sure that his simple analogy had been successful in putting over the concept, but was frustrated when the congressman responded, "That's all very well, Mr. Director, but I thought the Department of Agriculture took care of potatoes."

It was persistent and dedicated research that gave the Census Bureau its present highly sophisticated battery of sample survey designs. One of the early contributions was the advancement of the theory of sampling on the basis of a finite population, rather than treating such a population as a sample drawn from an infinite population. Once theory had been developed to apply to a finite population, the application of such theory gave measures of sampling error that were directly applicable to the population under study.

Another milestone was the evaluation of various methods of defining sampling units for area sampling and for stratifying them. This made it feasible to associate people, farms, business establishments, or other units with sampling units defined in terms of areas, and thereby to draw efficient probability samples without an adequate list of the target population. It was determined by the early 1940's that stratified samples of area units could effectively reflect changes over time as well as the situation at one point in time.

One of the problems attacked by the sampling staff concerned the development of a multistage design which provided for sufficient clustering of the sampling units to permit strong administrative and quality control. It was learned in the early investigations that, under certain conditions which were shown to hold in many cases, the use of primary sampling units consisting of counties or groups of adjacent counties could decrease the sampling variance more than it would increase the cost, provided these first stage units were selected with probability proportionate to size.

Another significant advance, already discussed—the development of rotating samples for retail trade and for the Current Population Survey—provided for partial replacement each month. This yielded both administrative and technical gains. The burden on the field organization was reduced by the device of having each small sampled area visited for a number of months, or in a special rotation pattern. Such a pattern took into account the limitation imposed by the reluctance of some households or stores to remain in a particular survey operation for an unduly protracted period. The

technical advantage of this plan of rotation is its ability to provide estimates of month-to-month and year-to-year changes,
thus yielding important information and increasing the efficiency of the estimating process.

An interesting development in survey sample design has
been the sharp increase in the number of primary sampling
units (PSU's) included in the sample, coupled with measures
to improve and systematize the span of supervisory control.
An early sample set up under WPA auspices was based on 68
PSU's, consisting of counties or pairs of counties. In each
PSU there was a resident supervisor with the capability of frequent close contact with the few enumerators working under
his jurisdiction. Appropriate sampling theory and empirical
studies of cost, of the components of sampling error, and of
supervisory methods, revealed that the level of sampling error
per unit cost could be considerably reduced by increasing the
number of PSU's, and reducing the sampling rates within the
PSU's, and that at the same time supervision could be
strengthened through the use of strong regional offices. Hence,
there took place a progressive increase in the number of such
units until it reached the present number of about 450 (partly
as a consequence of more than doubling the number of households included in the sample).

Estimation provides another example of the advances made
by research. Prior to the Census Bureau's pioneer work, the
standard method for making estimates based on a sample was
the use of simple linear estimates (for example, applying an
expansion factor of 100 uniformly to the results from a 1 per
cent sample). Because this method yielded estimates of unnecessarily low reliability, the theory of ratio estimates was
applied to a wide variety of the Bureau's surveys. Through
ratio estimation, it is possible to make use of independent information on the population, such as its distribution by age
and sex. Thus, the expansion factor is varied slightly from
one age-sex component to another, so that the age-sex distri-

bution of the expanded sample will conform to the independently determined totals for the universe from which the sample was drawn. Increasingly sophisticated estimating procedures appropriate to the current retail trade survey and the Current Population Survey include methods that take advantage of the rotation of the sample and the correlation between current and previous estimates from parts of the sample. Using these techniques, it has been possible to achieve gains in estimating efficiency equivalent to those that might have been secured by substantial increases in size of sample. These gains have been made feasible by the use of modern computers in applying complex estimation procedures.

Broadening of the Research and Development Function

During the 1940's, the major accomplishments of the research staff were in the field of sampling theory and its application to censuses and surveys. Toward the end of that decade, however, the staff began to make some progress in a second major area—the systematic analysis of the magnitude and over-all effect of survey errors arising from sources other than sampling, particularly response or measurement errors. The first stage of this analysis was based on results obtained from several postcensus evaluative surveys, using highly trained, carefully supervised interviewers, and special questionnaires and procedures.

The evaluation surveys led to significant changes in a number of the censuses to which they were applied. In their first use (the 1945 Census of Agriculture), they indicated the special difficulties in the identification of marginal farms, as well as in the enumeration of areas where nonresident farming is prevalent. When used in connection with the 1948 Census of Business, they demonstrated that the use of tax files as a source of mailing lists for all establishments with employees and as a substitute for the census in the case of very small units, such as those without paid employees, was superior to direct field canvassing for this type of census.

The postenumeration survey for the 1950 Census of Population and Housing represented a vigorous effort to measure the biases of the census by means of using much greater resources in training and canvassing. Even though the costs per case were about twenty times those for the census, the results from the intensive interviews were not greatly different for most items. In the case of income, however, there was a significant difference, with the more detailed questioning about income apparently yielding more accurate information.

For certain items it was possible to compare the results of the census with those of the Current Population Survey (CPS). The data on employment status from the two operations proved to be substantially different. The differences were large enough to be both statistically significant and economically important. If the more careful CPS process can be assumed to yield substantially true values for labor force participation and for unemployment, the census results for these items have a substantial bias.* This is not surprising, for some of the marginal members of the labor force can easily be overlooked by enumerators not fully trained about the need to ask the full series of labor force questions for each person to whom they apply.

Measurement of Nonsampling Errors

From the evaluation programs it has been learned that nonsampling errors are often of significant magnitude and may arise at a number of points in the operations of collection and processing. Some of the errors are of the sort that tend to cancel out and have an effect much like sampling variability; others, reflecting the influence of some systematic

* As noted in Chapter V, the same relationship was discovered in the comparison of the original WPA survey and the results of the 1940 census.

tendency, do not tend to cancel out and therefore produce response biases.

An important example of the effect of response variance was found in the impact that the choice of an individual enumerator may have upon the data for a particular area. This component of error, now known as enumerator variability, arises from the fact that the results obtained by the same enumerator at different households tend to be more alike than if they were obtained by different enumerators. As a result of randomizing certain enumerator assignments in connection with the 1950 census, it was discovered that the effect of enumerator variance can be large enough to raise the response standard deviation to a very substantial level. In fact, the variability introduced by enumerators was as large on the average as that which would have been introduced by a 25 per cent sample without enumerator variance.

The practical implications of this discovery have been very great. They broadened the acceptance of 25 per cent samples for quite small areas (such as census tracts of four thousand to five thousand population) by demonstrating that for many items the additional information in a 100 per cent census is not worth the added cost. Furthermore, they gave great impetus to the extension of self-enumeration as a means of eliminating most of the variance due to individual enumerators.

Tests of self-enumeration in connection with the 1950 and 1960 censuses were generally encouraging with respect both to rates and quality of response. The results of studies to determine the amount of response variation in connection with the self-enumeration approach also gave support to the adoption of this procedure.

After the 1960 census, careful estimates of the amount of underenumeration based on demographic analysis indicated that the real deficiency was probably about 3 per cent, rather than the 1.5 per cent shown by the postenumeration survey.

Even worse, from the viewpoint of many users, were the sharp differences in the rate of undercoverage for various segments of the population. This element of nonsampling error was clearly great enough to call for major attention in the over-all plans for 1970.

SURVEY DESIGN AND SYSTEMS ANALYSIS

With the rapid growth in knowledge about both sampling and nonsampling errors, it is natural that statistical production began to be regarded as an integrated process in the 1960's, from the original planning of content and methods to the final system for the delivery of data to the consumer. It had become clear that many different factors affect the quality of the output and that some can be dealt with more readily than others. On the other side of the coin, there are many routes to increasing efficiency in the production process, some of which are capable of more rapid realization than others. With so many alternative courses of action, it became clear that much research would continue to be required to approach the optimum output with fixed resources.

Self-Enumeration

In view of the clear evidence from the enumerator variance studies, there was a strong impetus to have as much as possible of the 1970 census carried out by mail. A series of some twenty-five tests, both large and small, showed that households could use a position-marking form successfully and that the average response rate of some 80 per cent would be high enough to warrant the use of the mails for collection, with enumerator follow-up as required because of nonresponse or errors. It was further decided to limit the approach to the larger metropolitan areas and some adjacent territory, including about 60 per cent of the total population. Tests revealed that the most economical approach would be to use commercial mailing lists where available, otherwise to depend upon the listing of addresses by census field personnel. The tests further indicated that the postal employees could very successfully correct and update the commercial lists, adding new cards to the file for all missing units and eliminating cards for units no longer in existence.

Coverage Improvement

The shift to self-enumeration for as little as 60 per cent of the population could be expected to yield substantial improvement in coverage, by reducing that part of the undercoverage due to the omission of complete dwelling units or structures. The ability of the local postal carriers to remedy the deficiencies of the lists with which they started gave assurance of better coverage of structures than had previously been achieved by enumerators. Particular emphasis was placed upon the ghetto areas, where a group of some twenty community specialists were recruited in order to help gain the confidence of the people living in these areas. (Other aspects of the publicity program will be described in Chapter XII.) There was also more intensive training and closer supervision of all the personnel working in the difficult areas. Among the other devices used to strengthen coverage was a special check of all persons who moved during the period of the census. In sixteen states, a postenumerative check was carried out by postal employees to ascertain the completeness of the lists that had been compiled by the census field staff.

DATA DELIVERY SYSTEMS; THE ECONOMIC CENSUSES

In the mid-1960's, the Bureau's first Small Area Data Advisory Committee was created and promptly began to stress the need for greater flexibility in providing data for small geographic areas. Fortunately, the proven capabilities of electronic computers were such as to open the way to substantial improvement in the services offered to users of census data. Since many users, both public and private, were already equipped to use information in the form of summary tapes directly from computers, it was feasible to plan on a very great increase in this form of data delivery.

A major step in expanding the capability of the Bureau to meet small area needs was the coding of addresses in urbanized areas, so that the computer could allocate an individual unit to a geographic area as small as one side of a block. This capability makes it possible to group census results in terms of any combination of sides of blocks. An additional capability involves the determination of geographic coordinates applying to street intersections and certain other points. The ability to associate this information with addresses in the computer makes it possible to determine the number of households of a particular type (for example, households with income above a certain level) that are within five miles of a proposed shopping center.

Users are enabled also to take advantage of the possibility of graphic presentation of data. With the assignment of coordinates to street intersections and with census data in machine-readable form, the analyst can use the computer for aggregating and cross-correlating many kinds of urban data for specific locations or specific areas.

The contributions of research and development have been as important to the economic censuses as to the demographic censuses. Reference has already been made to the use of administrative records as a source of mailing lists and as a means of providing the data from smaller business units that were formerly collected by census schedules. Another development important for the economic censuses has been the use of the computer to detect and correct many of the errors in the returns. The ability of the computer to analyze the relationships among the major elements of a return gives it a great advantage over a clerk in identifying the most probable explanation for an inconsistency or error and in determining the adjustment that is most likely, on the average, to be the right one. The computer will also identify large discrepancies that require further contact with the respondent.

PRODUCTIVITY

For all their emphasis upon measurement, statisticians in the Census Bureau have not provided much quantitative evidence on gains in productivity arising from advances in technology. Only indirect and fragmentary evidence is available to suggest that sharp gains have been made possible by the development of new equipment and by the advances in statistical technology.

One type of evidence is provided by the fact that in man-year terms, the resources applied to the censuses have decreased in the past two decades. When this fact is considered against the background of new subject areas covered, such as income, labor force measurement in detail, place of work, and the like, the great increase in the number of blocks, tracts, and other small areas for which data are provided, the sharp expansion in the number of publication pages, the greater timeliness of the results, and the greater emphasis upon measuring and improving quality of results, it is clear that productivity gains have been impressive. One dramatic indication of this is the reduction in personnel required for processing the decennial census. The peak employment of temporary clerical personnel has been reduced about 50 per cent over the past two censuses, with an especially impressive reduction in the number of persons required for card-punching work. At the same time, most results were published at a much earlier date.

Another case that has been documented more fully is furnished by the economic censuses in the 1950's, when the already demonstrated usefulness of administrative records

TABLE VIII

Productivity and Cost Improvement—Economic Censuses, 1947–67

Censuses [a]	Total Obligations (thousands of dollars)	Establishments Covered (thousands)	Cost per Establishment Covered (dollars)	Index of Productivity in Constant Dollars per Establishment Covered (1948 = 100%)
1947–48 Business/Manufactures				
Actual	$17,589	2,922	6.02	100%
At current prices	42,581	2,922	14.57	
1954 Censuses				
Actual	13,748	3,099	4.44	177%
At current prices	25,441	3,099	8.21	
1958 Censuses				
Actual	15,648	3,402	4.60	197%
At current prices	25,156	3,402	7.39	
1963 Censuses				
Actual	19,542	3,592	5.44	204%
At current prices	25,616	3,592	7.13	
1967 Censuses				
Actual	22,662	4,826	4.70	279%
At current prices	25,229	4,826	5.23	

[a] Census of minerals included in 1954, 1958, 1963, and 1967. Merchandise lines included only in 1948, 1963, and 1967. Census of transportation included only in 1963 and 1967. Contract construction, lawyers, travel agencies, architects and engineers are included only in 1967.

paved the way for some highly important changes in technology. Table VIII shows the per schedule cost of the censuses of business over the twenty-year period 1947–67. It will be noted that even in actual costs, the outlay per establishment declined by some 20 per cent. In terms of current dollars, the decrease was well over 60 per cent. This illustrates the dramatic gain resulting from a conjunction of three developments: the creation of a dependable mailing list so that enumerators were no longer needed; the use of administrative records to provide information for smaller business units (those without paid employees); and the effective use of electronic computers to do some of the jobs formerly handled by clerks. The table cannot be projected to show longtime rates of gain in productivity, but it does reveal the very large payoff from a research and development program.

VIII

Census Tools—and Toolmakers

The tasks performed by the Census Bureau every ten years have been so different from those performed by other statistical agencies that commercial equipment and methods have often not been adequate. Two outstanding break-throughs in large-scale data processing—first the punched card system and later electronic computers—both received initial impetus from inside the Census Bureau. From 1910 to 1950, equipment built by the Bureau's machine shop was substantially more productive for census work than any equipment available commercially. During the next twenty years, the most satisfactory approach to the problem of transferring information from large census-type schedules to magnetic tapes used by electronic computers was developed by the Bureau itself, with the help of the technical staff of the National Bureau of Standards.

THE PUNCHED CARD ERA

Prior to 1890, the summarization of census results had been accomplished by tally sheets. Some advances had been made, to be sure, in the 1870 and 1880 censuses by the so-called Seaton device, developed by Charles W. Seaton, who became Superintendent of the Census in 1881. This was a simple wooden contrivance comprising sixteen rollers set in two tiers 6 or 8 inches apart over which a long roll of paper was conducted in such fashion that tally marks or figures entered on the tops of the upper tier of rollers would appear, when the paper was unrolled, in solid blocks readily counted or in columns convenient for addition.

The beginning of the punched card era can be traced to the cooperation between two men in the Census office in the early years following the 1880 census. Herman Hollerith, a young engineer, was employed as a special agent, and Dr. John Shaw Billings was in charge of the Division of Vital Statistics. The most generally accepted account of the origin is that Dr. Billings suggested to Hollerith that there ought to be some mechanical way of tabulating the results of a census. Hollerith became interested in the idea, left the government in 1883, and, by the time of the 1890 census, had developed and tested a tabulating machine. This machine had its first large-scale application in that census and with only minor modifications was used also in the 1900 census and for a part of the work in 1910.

In 1903, shortly after the creation of the permanent Bureau, Simon N. D. North concluded that the rates charged by Hollerith's company were excessive. In 1905 North refused to renew the contract and obtained $40,000 from Congress for experimental work in developing tabulation machinery. In 1907, the activity was transferred from quarters furnished by the Bureau of Standards to space in the Bureau of the Census, where it was to function continuously to the present day as the Engineering and Development Laboratory, serving not only the Bureau, but also many other agencies of the government. In 1910, the Tabulating Machine Company brought a suit against the Director of the Census, claiming infringement of patents, and the shop could easily have become a casualty of one of the periodic drives to reduce government activity and to have private industry supply goods and services. In recent years, with the truly enormous research facilities available in many of the larger companies, it has been possible to make a strong argument that a Bureau machine shop, dependent for much of its equipment upon government surplus stocks, could not possibly achieve results as rapidly or as efficiently as private companies, but fortunately none of these considerations has prevailed, and the continuation of the Engineering and Development Laboratory has yielded a number of dramatic payoffs.*

From 1910 to 1950, much of the Bureau's punching, sorting, and tabulating equipment was built or modified in its

---

* In its more than sixty years of operation, the laboratory has produced a wide range of equipment and services. One example—the automatic microfilming machine—will suffice to illustrate the kinds of contribution made by this organization. The microfilming of the 1970 Population and Housing Schedules imposed volume and time requirements unequaled in any previous undertaking of this kind. First, it was necessary in about three months to produce an acceptable image of some 70 million documents applying to all households. In the case of the sample schedules, the total work load was about the same or a little larger, since the average sample schedule called for a little more than five frames. The automatic filming of the sample forms was complicated by the fact that the pages had to be turned in order to get a complete record for each household.

Anthony Berlinsky conceived the idea for constructing an automatic microfilming machine, which was designed, tested, modified as necessary, and constructed in final form under his immediate direction. The forty machines constructed by the laboratory were installed and used in the Operations Office in Jeffersonville, Indiana. They had the capability of feeding in and moving schedules on a perforated Mylar-vacuum-belt bed, stopping them at the precise point required under a modified high-speed camera, and then moving them along to a point where they were once again put in stack form. The sample data, in small booklets rather than single-sheet forms, were handled at the rate of about sixty pages per minute. The pages were turned by a vacuum head mounted on a rotating arm, which passed over the booklet as soon as it had reached the proper position on the Mylar belt. The vacuum head picked up a corner of the top page and brushed the page flat for microfilming, while another rotating arm with a similar vacuum head moved to pick up the next page. When the last page was reached, the machine received a signal that caused it to eject and stack the completed forms.

machine shop. The heart of the system was the census unit counter, a device uniquely suited to the requirements of the census, where so much of the work consists of counting the number of individuals or dwelling units having certain characteristics. Until nearly 1950, the basic machine was altered relatively little, although a number of improvements were made.

The unit counters used for the 1940 census were heavy, utilitarian pieces of equipment, completely lacking any aesthetic appeal, in sharp contrast to today's streamlined chrome- and plastic-covered machines. Until the mid-1940's, the complicated interconnections required for carrying out each census count were made by means of a network of fine wires soldered to the appropriate terminals.

In the late 1940's, there were a number of significant advances in the tabulating equipment constructed in the Bureau's shops. One development was the multicolumn sorter, capable of sorting cards on the basis of the combination of information from a number of columns, rather than from a single column. The unit counter was further improved for the 1950 census. At about the same time the International Business Machines Corporation (IBM) announced a new series of equipment, particularly designed for census-type work in the United States and foreign countries. This new series, the 101, had capabilities similar to a combination of the unit counter and the multicolumn sorter. It was apparently a direct result of the transfer to IBM of Lawrence Wilson, who had served as chief of the Census Bureau's Machine Tabulation Division. It is somewhat ironic that these substantial gains in conventional equipment came at the dawn of the electronic era of mass tabulation.*

* For more detail on all matters connected with the early history of tabulation in the Bureau of the Census, the reader is referred to Leon E. Truesdell, *The Development of Punch Card Tabulation in the Bureau of the Census, 1890–1940,* Washington: Government Printing Office, 1965.

THE COMPUTER ERA

In the 1940's, it became evident that the punched card system, despite some gains in speed and sophistication, was unable to keep abreast of the new censuses and surveys, the greater number of inquiries, and the increased complexity of tabulations called for by users. The question naturally arose as to whether a solution might be found in the electronic computers, which had been used with great success for tasks requiring long and detailed computations, such as those connected with ballistics and atomic research. All of the earliest computers were of the type that came to be known as "scientific computers." They were designed to carry out a long series of operations on a relatively small amount of data, whereas for the data processing of the census, it would be necessary to reverse the emphasis and carry out limited operations on an enormous input.

The first step was taken in the fall of 1946, when the Bureau arranged to have the National Bureau of Standards study the feasibility of adapting electronic computers to statistical data processing. The prospects were encouraging, and in 1948 the Bureau of Standards contracted with the Eckert-Mauchly Computer Corporation for a general-purpose electronic digital computing system, known as the UNIVAC system, designed to fit the needs of the Bureau of the Census.

In April, 1951, the first UNIVAC was delivered. The speeds of computer operation then, though modest in terms of later electronic equipment, were far in advance of those achieved by the punched card system. An important feature of UNIVAC I, as well as of subsequent computers, is the reading head, which is able to transfer to and from a metallic tape information expressed on the tape as a combination of magnetized spots. UNIVAC I could transfer letters or digits to and from tape at the rate of 10,000 per second and at the same time perform operations, such as adding or comparing numbers, at the rate of 2,000 per second. Since the new computer staff had prepared the necessary computer instructions to carry out a part of the 1950 census, the new machine was promptly put to work on a round-the-clock schedule seven days a week. It was used on the 1950 tabulations for only a few states, but the experience gained during this period proved invaluable. One of the lessons learned from this was that success in applying a computer to data processing requires complete re-evaluation of standards, procedures, and philosophy.

After the 1950 census, the application of the computer to the Bureau's current surveys showed its advantages over conventional equipment. Time schedules were shortened, and the dollar cost of data processing was typically, but not uniformly, reduced by about 50 per cent. In the mid-1950's a satisfactory high-speed printer and an efficient device for converting punched cards to magnetic tape were added to the system. With these advances and the acquisition of a second UNIVAC I, the Bureau was ready to apply the new system to the 1954 economic censuses.

By 1956, with the next decennial census just around the corner, it was time to consider the next steps toward expansion of capacity. On the basis of a careful review, the conclusion was reached that the best choice of equipment would be a so-called scientific computer, modified to meet the specifications of the Bureau—a machine that was eventually designated the 1105. The Bureau acquired two 1105's for work on the 1957 series of economic censuses and then later arranged a contract with two universities to provide the additional capacity that would be needed for the 1960 census. Although the new computers had internal speeds about ten times that of the UNIVAC I, in practice the realized gain was substantially lower.

As the third generation of computers became available in

the 1960's, a review by an outside committee led to the decision that the Bureau should shift to the UNIVAC 1107 series of computers. The first 1107 was acquired in 1963, and the closely related higher-speed version, the UNIVAC 1108, was added in 1967. For the work on the 1970 census, the Bureau had the services of two 1107's and two 1108's, as well as additional units of much smaller capacity but with the ability to replace the more expensive machines for certain types of jobs. For the new 1108's, the magnetic tape units can read from or write on magnetic tape at the rate of 120,000 characters per second, or twelve times the corresponding rate for UNIVAC I. The new machine can carry out instructions (such as adding two numbers and recording the result) at the rate of 1.3 million instructions per second, or 600 times the corresponding rate for the first machine.

The guidelines that the Bureau has followed in acquiring and maintaining its electronic equipment are generally different from those of many other agencies, both government and private. It has almost always purchased rather than rented equipment. Usually the full-time operation of a computer makes it possible to return the cost in rental savings within less than three years.

Coupled with this is the policy of relatively slow turnover of major pieces of equipment. Generally the period of active service for a particular model is eight to ten years, but in the case of the original UNIVAC I, formal retirement came at the age of twelve.

A third feature of Bureau policy has been the maintenance of all the equipment that it purchases. Not only has this proved to be definitely economical, but it has also paved the way for Bureau engineers to introduce modifications in line with special needs. Furthermore, at times when contracts for new units are being negotiated, it gives the Bureau a basis for attesting to the feasibility of innovations in the standard line that the company has been producing.

The Problem of Input

From the time the first UNIVAC was acquired, the problems of input and output equipment have been vexing and continuous. The increase in internal computing speeds has put pressure upon managers of electronic systems to learn how to move data into and out of the computer at speeds commensurate with the internal capacity. The problem of output was soon met by improvements in high-speed printers and the ability to run them on an "off-line" basis, without tying up the central computer's time.

The input problem is much more difficult and will not be completely solved unless equipment can be developed to read both typed and handwritten characters.

During the 1940's, steps were taken to see whether IBM or some other company might develop a capability for direct transfer of information from a larger form, on which information had been recorded by position marking. Tests undertaken by the Census staff revealed that information recorded in this manner would equal in quality that recorded by conventional procedures. In 1948, the IBM Corporation, which had given considerable engineering attention to the census needs, concluded that it could not complete the design and production of equipment in time for the 1950 census.

In 1949, the Bureau of the Census once more turned to the National Bureau of Standards for assistance, and in 1953 the first piece of equipment was delivered to the Census Bureau. It was known as FOSDIC, an acronym for Film Optical Sensing Device for Input to Computers. Through its application to several fairly large census undertakings, its speed and reliability were demonstrated. An improved model, FOSDIC III, served as a prototype for the four production models that were later used for the 1960 census. The results were most gratifying. Seven months were saved in the completion of input for processing by the census tabulators. The net saving amounted to more than $5 million, and the equipment was available for other tasks of the Bureau.

The 1970 census, with its use of individual schedules for each household, required an improved version of FOSDIC. The units developed for this census are controlled by internally stored programs and are capable of performing data edits and computations through a small but extremely rapid computer. They can process 450 frames of microfilm per minute, doing in 15 seconds what the 1960 machine could do in 60, and what a punched card operator would have taken 8 hours to accomplish in 1950. It is estimated that the 1970 savings over punching amounted to $10 million.

It would be a mistake to think of such developments solely in terms of savings realized in time and cost, for their full impact cannot be measured in this way. The use of computers to do tasks formerly carried out by clerks has led to a higher degree of accuracy for many operations and has made it possible to introduce kinds of review that would have been out of the question for clerks. This is particularly true in the field of estimation from sample results and in the editing and imputation applied to defective returns. Computers and associated equipment have also made great contributions to the efficiency with which samples can be designed and administered.

IX

The Creed of a Statistical Agency

The title of this chapter uses a term that ordinarily connotes the set of beliefs held by a religious organization. The use of the word "creed" is deliberate because it best conveys the zeal and dedication with which the staff of the Bureau has created, extended, and followed a consistent set of principles. The antecedents of some of the elements of the creed go back at least one hundred years, but the development of most of the other elements is due largely to the rise in professionalism that began shortly before World War II.

MEASUREMENT

It is natural that the first element in the creed of a statistical agency is a belief in the importance of objective measurement. In the case of the Census Bureau, this has been applied to a wide range of social and economic phenomena.

In carrying out the central function of measurement, the Bureau has moved into new fields and has developed current data in most of the areas covered by the censuses. Extensive research and testing have been required in a number of new fields, such as income, labor force, consumer buying intentions, and alterations and repairs carried out by homeowners. In new fields, especially, the task of setting up definitions and clarifying conceptual matters must have been completed in advance of setting up a statistical inquiry. Much work in sampling and response research has been needed in order to enable the Bureau to provide measures of current changes without undue costs. The design of efficient samples of persons, households, and economic enterprises has been essential to the whole program of measuring change on a monthly, quarterly, or annual basis as needed for current decisions by business and government. The emphasis at all times has been to utilize modern sampling theory and the results of response research in such a manner as to ensure objective and unbiased results. The goal of improved measurement has led to much examination of means of improving the rate of response on all censuses and surveys and of reducing the burden upon respondents without sacrifice of quality.

Perhaps the outstanding indication of the Bureau's devotion to measurement is the attention it has given in recent years to obtaining measures of the accuracy of its measurements. It has become a consistent policy to provide as regularly as possible a measure of the accuracy of all censuses and surveys and to do the same for the work performed for other agencies. An important reason for the development of probability samples of population, dwelling units, and business establishments was their ability to yield measures of errors for all the Bureau's data from sample surveys.

THE SEARCH FOR BETTER METHODS

One of the methods the Bureau has long used to find resources to extend the scope of its measurement operations has been to develop better procedures for carrying out its regular census and surveys. Over the years, this has been a lonely task, for many of the operations of the Bureau differ so greatly in magnitude and character from those performed by other agencies, either public or private, that completely new equipment and methods may have to be devised in the light of operating requirements. Examples of innovation in connection with mechanical and electronic tabulating equipment have been noted in the preceding chapter.

The search for better methods of carrying out the census mission has not been limited to equipment development. Among the outstanding examples of procedural changes in recent years are the increased use of administrative records in lieu of special questionnaires and the collecting of more and more of the census information by mail rather than direct canvass. In both cases there have been significant gains in quality of results as well as an increase in productivity. The use of mail instead of direct canvass was an important contribution to quality improvement in the 1970 census. To put the population census on a mail-out/mail-back basis, it was necessary to carry out extensive testing on two fronts: (1) the feasibility of using commercial address lists, when brought up to date and corrected by local postal workers; and (2) the ability and willingness of householders to fill out self-coding forms.

The Bureau's emphasis upon improving methods is further indicated by its use of production standards in a major part of all its clerical operations. By this method, tasks are broken down into small components, for each of which the normal time needed is determined. Despite the fact that production standards have made substantial savings, they have not been widely used in other statistical agencies. One exception is the Swedish Central Bureau of Statistics, where there has been much emphasis upon the rationalization of statistical production.

The Bureau staff has always been highly pragmatic in its search for better methods. Extensive experimental work and testing have been involved in every improvement introduced.

Often a new approach is tested, even when it runs counter to conventional wisdom. An example is provided by the FOSDIC schedule, requiring the answering of questions by putting marks in certain positions. Conventional wisdom—the author's included—suggested that such a form would be suitable for use by specially trained enumerators but not by household members preparing their own returns. The research staff believed that a form of this type could be designed for household use and proved they were right by a series of tests. Their final vindication came with the 1970 census, when such forms were filled out successfully for most of the population.

CANDOR REGARDING PRODUCT AND METHODS

Another element of the creed of a statistical agency is the provision of full information regarding its work, including evaluation of accuracy and full description of methods. In this era, when the interests of consumers are receiving particular attention, this may seem a minimum acceptance of responsibility. As a matter of fact, the adoption of this policy in the mid-1940's constituted a marked break from the time-honored point of view that "if it's in the census, it's right." Superintendent of the Census Francis A. Walker was far ahead of his time in 1871, when he recognized the duty of the producers of statistics to be candid about their shortcomings, even though as a consequence the results of the census might receive less credit. Walker probably did not foresee that the ultimate result of admitting and measuring errors is an increase in the credibility of all of the agency's work.

Many, although not all, of the Bureau's bulletins and releases include a certain amount of what might be called descriptive analysis. This may involve informing the reader about other related data, regardless of source, and may call his attention to definitions, coverage, or other factors which should be taken into account in relating two or more sets of data. On the other hand, economic and social analysis, needed as a basis for policy conclusions and recommendations, is not undertaken in the usual census reports. Such boundaries for the Bureau's work are consistent with the Office of Management and Budget directive mentioned in Chapter II.

An illustration of the policy of reporting on methods is furnished by the Research Documentation Repository, which contains a mixture of memoranda, forms, instructions, status reports and research results. This repository is systematically reviewed in order to identify those materials that should be published as well as those that would be useful to workers outside of the Bureau but do not merit formal publication. The inclusion of negative, as well as positive research results, is often useful to those in other agencies and in foreign governments facing problems similar to those encountered in the Bureau.

EMPHASIS ON THE PUBLIC INTEREST

A fourth tenet of faith long observed in Bureau operations is an unremitting devotion to what it believes is in the public interest. As an agency within a Department, it has endeavored to function primarily as a general-purpose service agency of the entire government and only secondarily as an organization supporting the departmental mission. It has developed a tradition for making extraordinary efforts to develop its program as responsibly as possible to meet public needs and to take full advantage of the economies of operation that have been made possible by recent improvements in the state of the art.

Some examples of unusual efforts, with the usual conflict over any innovation, can be cited in connection with each of the last four decennial censuses. In 1940, the Bureau faced much controversy and criticism because of its decision to put some of the inquiries on a sample basis, and because of the introduction of income questions as well as a new battery of inquiries to collect employment data according to the new labor force approach. For the 1950 census, sampling, although not yet fully accepted by all users, was used much more extensively and a series of completely new statistical areas were set up, including Standard Metropolitan Statistical Areas and urbanized areas. The 1950 census was the first in which a special postenumeration survey was conducted. This was also the year in which some of the census was first tabulated by an electronic computer.

Perhaps the two most significant innovations for the 1960 census were the much fuller use of sampling and the procedure of having sample householders fill out their own long-form questionnaires. Again, in the 1970 census, there were further significant changes from earlier procedures. For about 60 per cent of the country, the census was conducted on a full mail-out/mail-back basis. In addition, families were required for the first time to use a self-coding form of schedule so that microfilm copies might be read directly by the Bureau's special equipment. Finally, data for the census of agriculture were collected by mail for the first time in 1969 through the use of mailing lists derived from tax returns and other administrative records.

DEALING WITH ISSUES

Most creeds involve conflicts in application, and that of the Census Bureau is no exception. Some examples of particular issues may serve to illustrate the complexity of the problems of a statistical service agency. Fixing the boundaries of the Bureau's mission is one of the troublesome recurring questions. For example, the Bureau may be requested to undertake a reimbursable job that is marginal to the Bureau's mission and that in some cases has little or no statistical content. There are no firm rules for cases of this type, but one element to consider would be the possibility of adding to the stock of knowledge about census and survey methods.

Another issue in taking account of the public interest involves the choice between (1) the introduction of new or modified inquiries and (2) adherence to the old measures in the interest of maintaining comparability with the past. Those who favor the new measures often do so because of changing phenomena to be measured. In view of economic or social changes, they stress the need for making improvements as rapidly as possible to lay the basis for better measures of present levels. Those who favor comparability as a primary goal emphasize the importance of being able to interpret changes over a period of years. Here again, no definite rule can be set up, but the Bureau has tended to adopt improved measures when they have been adequately tested to establish their feasibility. At the same time, it has always endeavored to furnish some kind of overlap so as to give an estimate of the change in level due to the new definition.

Sometimes an issue arises that requires compromise among three somewhat conflicting goals: (1) speed in reporting results, (2) cost reduction, and (3) maintenance of high quality. Speeding up the first report to the public may be accomplished by special attention to the respondents, by increasing the size of the processing force, or by basing the initial tabulations upon partial returns. Some of these steps are at variance with the goals of reducing costs and improving quality. Reduction of costs in statistical surveys, assuming that normal efficiencies have already been achieved, may take the form of reducing the size of a sample or of evening out the work load by prolonging the processing period. These actions will have adverse effects upon either timeliness or quality. The third objective, quality, may call for a larger sample, or more intensive training of the field organization, or some modification of the processing procedures. Such changes are likely to involve greater costs and increase the time required for the production of statistics. In practice, there is no general basis for dealing with a series of alternatives like these. As useful a device as any may be a cost-benefit approach, in which a series of alternatives is laid out, with varying assumptions about cost, timeliness, and quality.

In summary, there are many conflicts in the planning and production of statistical data. The search for guiding principles will continue, but the statistical administrator will always be subject to complaints, criticism, and letters to the editor. His decisions can never satisfy all users, but, at the same time, he will seldom lose all his supporters.

The Bureau and Other Government Agencies

The Census Bureau's role as a service agency brings it into many recurring relationships with government agencies, a number of which have already been described. This chapter will deal with other relationships, some resulting from organizational or legislative provisions and others being a natural outgrowth of the historical role of the Bureau.

Relationships with Federal Agencies

The Census Bureau, as a general statistical service agency, is not a really logical component of any of the existing departments of the government. The fact that in its long history it has successively been a part of the departments of State, Interior, Commerce and Labor, and finally Commerce is perhaps the best indication that the mission of the Bureau is not uniquely associated with that of any one of the departments. Because of the lack of any unique community of interest between the Bureau and any of the departments in which it has been located, it is not surprising that as a rule it has been given a good deal of independence in carrying out its tasks. Indeed, the legislative history of the development of the Census Bureau as a permanent organization reinforces the distinctive and separate role of this institution. It was not until recodification of the statutes in 1954 (see Appendix D) that the duties, responsibilities, and powers assigned to the Director of the Census by law were restated as attributes of the Secretary of Commerce as a part of a general standardization of legislative treatment of the departments and their constituent agencies.

The Department of Commerce

For many years, the Bureau was under the immediate direction of an assistant secretary with little or no knowledge of the Bureau's function and role. Therefore, even in the field of budget preparation, the Department furnished little direct guidance and support for the Bureau's program.

In the light of this long period of mutual noninvolvement, it is easy to see why the Bureau was so vulnerable to the influence of Secretary of Commerce Sinclair Weeks, who came into office in 1953 with an expressed intention to clear out the "deadwood and poison oak," which he thought had accumulated. He believed that substantial economies could be effected in statistical work; his service as Board Chairman of Reed and Barton Corporation had apparently given him no familiarity with the business uses of Bureau of Census data.

Shortly after Weeks became Secretary, the major appropriations for the 1953 economic censuses were scheduled to be sent forward to the Congress. He first questioned the need for this activity. When he learned that these censuses are mandatory under census legislation, he forwarded the request with a clear indication that the Congress should decide the fate of the censuses. In this case, a seemingly neutral position amounted to an invitation to cut, which was quickly accepted by the Congress. The reactions of business and other users were violent and prompt, and the Secretary decided to appoint an Intensive Review Committee to appraise all census programs. The committee, consisting mainly of business economists and statisticians, started its deliberations in October, 1953, and completed its work by the following February. The committee strongly supported the economic censuses and recommended that the censuses originally planned for 1953 be carried out one year later and that henceforward these censuses should be continued in accordance with the original schedule, that is for years ending in *3* and *8*.

One by-product of the 1953–54 review and delay in executing the censuses was the formation of the Federal Statistics Users' Conference, a group of business, farm, labor, and research users of federal data, who keep in touch with the total federal statistical program and who act promptly when important series of data are in danger. Although it was conceived as a device for eliminating the need for a future rescue operation, such as the one conducted in 1953–54, it has proved extremely useful in promoting high standards, timeliness, and responsiveness in the federal statistical system.

A period of considerably closer working relationships with the Department of Commerce began early in 1963, when the reorganization of the Secretary's office provided for a new top official, the assistant secretary for Economic Affairs, to provide direct supervision over the Office of Business Economics and the Census Bureau. As of January 1, 1972, the assistant secretary for Economic Affairs was designated as administrator of the Social and Economic Statistics Administration, and the Office of Business Economics was redesignated as the Bureau of Economic Analysis. The series of officials who have served as assistant secretary or administrator since 1963 have been business economists already thoroughly familiar with the Census Bureau's work, including its historic role as a service agency for the entire government. This has been helpful in the Departmental review of proposals each year, since they have been able to bring direct high-level support for those programs that are not a part of the immediate mission of the

Department. Counteracting this, the closer integration has brought census budget proposals into much more direct competition with other Departmental initiatives. The government-wide character of the census mission includes some programs that have little relation to the program goals of the Commerce Department.

The thrust of the Department of Commerce has been directed toward a unified concept of all its activities, even to the extent of submerging the identity of the constituent bureaus with their highly distinctive roles and characters. It is doubtlessly true that, from the Secretary's viewpoint, the image of the Department is strengthened if the public can be made continuously aware of the Department's responsibility for all the undertakings within its jurisdiction. Unfortunately, this can be done only at the risk of some damage to the public understanding of the objectivity of the work of the scientific bureaus. The Department of Commerce is generally understood to have a business and trade orientation. Thus, when the independent image of a scientific bureau is subordinated to the Departmental image, questions may arise as to the objectivity of the work performed by that bureau. In the case of the Census Bureau, the objectivity of choice of subject matter for censuses and surveys may come to be regarded with suspicion.

Even in the release of data, many will erroneously take it for granted that nonscientific influences will sometimes affect the manner of release and relative emphasis in statistical analysis with regard to the reporting of data. To date, the releases of scientific statistical agencies like the Census and the former Office of Business Economics have been largely free of this kind of suspicion and the agency names constitute credentials of objectivity that are known and accepted by the public. The actual statistical reports are, of course, entirely clear as to the originating office. It is a disservice to the public, however, when Departmental press release arrangements are such that the name of the originating Bureau is omitted from published news stories.

Integration into a Departmental mission subjects a general service agency like the Census Bureau to certain other handicaps, as well. Always under some pressure to assure customer agencies that their work will be accorded full and adequate priority, the Census Bureau's ability to sustain such commitments in the face of conflicting Departmental priorities becomes less obvious and less credible to such agencies as the emphasis upon Departmental missions becomes more pronounced. There is almost a trusteeship role involved for the Census Bureau since major statistical undertakings and program responsibilities of numerous other agencies are entrusted to the Bureau's execution and are dependent on the Bureau's undivided commitment.

The Office of Management and Budget

Since the Office of Management and Budget (OMB—formerly the Bureau of the Budget) includes the coordinating mechanism known as the Statistical Policy Division, it has many and close relationships with the Census Bureau. Even if there were no agency for coordination, the Bureau of the Census, by virtue of its important service role in government, would wish to avoid initiating statistical inquiries without giving consideration to the same questions as those brought up by OMB. These include duplication of the work of other agencies, establishment of standards and concepts used in statistical surveys, and means of evaluating and sifting the varied needs of all federal agencies.

Working in close cooperation with OMB, Census is continually seeking to ensure that no data collection program, whether a part of its own work or carried out for other agencies, involves any avoidable overlap with existing programs. Consideration is given not only to purely statistical agencies, but also to agencies that collect data on such subjects as stocks, production, imports, and payrolls needed for regulation and administration in such areas as taxation, agricultural assistance, and conservation of natural resources. Whenever usable figures are available for some segment of a field, the Bureau of the Census endeavors to limit its direct collection to the minimum amount required to fill in the gaps. The continued surveillance of all collection efforts by OMB, and the resistance of respondents to furnish the same information to two or more agencies have eliminated the obvious cases of overlap. In cases where two agencies collect information from the same respondents, there must be a limited amount of duplication since both agencies require certain basic information in order to ensure proper identification of the unit supplying the figures.

The moderate degree of overlapping of identifying information is not the most serious problem when two departments at different times collect information from the same class of respondents, and in many cases from the same respondents. More serious may be the additional cost because mailing lists, sampling designs, and follow-up machinery of essentially the same type are maintained by two agencies. An example is furnished by the monthly collection of employment and payroll statistics by the Bureau of Labor Statistics, frequently through state labor departments, and the collection of data on industrial production, stocks, shipments, the volume of retail sales, and service receipts by the Census Bureau. If these collection functions could be integrated, the usefulness of the resulting statistics would be increased. Since the statistics could be matched, establishment by establishment, it would be possible to relate input and output figures for identical units and thus improve the measurement of productivity and strengthen economic analysis generally.

The Office of Management and Budget performs a valuable service for the Census Bureau by furnishing a means of channeling and evaluating all the federal agency needs for statistical information. For example, several years in advance of the decennial census, a Federal Council is organized by OMB to provide a focal point for bringing together and discussing all of the statistical needs within the government. In helping to establish priorities and in dealing with requests that lie outside the potentialities of the census, OMB can be extremely helpful. Ordinarily the limits imposed by over-all budgets, length of form, and public acceptance of certain kinds of inquiries lead to agreement on the part of the officials at the working levels, but in an exceptional situation, the differences of opinion can be so firmly held as to require final adjudication between the Secretary of Commerce and the director of OMB.

The role of OMB becomes particularly difficult when it believes that a statistical program originally proposed by the Census Bureau and supported by the Department should be replaced by a completely different proposal. In a number of cases in the past, such replacements have often involved the addition of a program notably useful for the Council of Economic Advisers as a substitute for one that was originally chosen within the Department. Thus, for example, the addition of improved measures of retail trade and of retail inventories has led to the displacement of Departmental programs for the improvement of some phase of the foreign trade statistics and of additional data on industrial commodities.

OMB carries out an important role in the development of standard classifications of commodities, occupations, industries, and geographic areas and the standardization of definitions and concepts. Because of its role in providing benchmark totals in major subject areas, the Census Bureau was one of the first agencies to face the problem of developing methods of classification and standard operating procedures that would permit meaningful comparisons of data from various sources. Thus, early impetus toward standardization was provided by the Bureau. Later, with the establishment of a coordinating mechanism in OMB, there was specific legislative provision for the establishment of standards for the statistical work of the government. In accordance with this, OMB has taken a major role in successive revisions of the Standard Industrial Classification (SIC). The first step in this operation was the creation of an interagency technical committee to review proposed changes in various industrial fields. The amendments proposed by this committee are reviewed by two advisory groups working with OMB—the Advisory Council on Federal Reports (for business) and the Labor Advisory Committee—but the final responsibility for deciding upon the classification to be submitted to OMB rests with the interagency committee.

Another major undertaking has been the establishment of SMSA's (Standard Metropolitan Statistical Areas), including all of the larger cities of the country. This program has frequently evoked controversy because some cities regard this kind of recognition as a mark of special prestige or as a requirement to assure local progress. Local officials are quick to challenge the validity of standards that lead to the exclusion of the one area important to them. Trips to Washington, D.C., by local delegations and congressional intervention are means frequently employed to emphasize reasons for an exception. In exercising its authority and responsibility in this field, OMB becomes a buffer against local pressures that may originally have been directed against the Census Bureau.

Definitions and concepts often require interagency consideration, and here again OMB has played an important role. For example, the labor force concepts are of concern to several agencies and have been the object of extensive study over many years by an interagency committee under OMB chairmanship. Similar attention, although on a less formal basis, has been given to the development of standard concepts and definitions in such fields as agriculture, income, and education to ensure that the work done by the Census Bureau will have maximum usefulness throughout the government.

Special Cooperative Arrangements

The Census Bureau has entered into a number of special arrangements with other federal agencies, usually with the active interest and support of the Office of Management and Budget. These arrangements have included the intensive use of administrative records and the central publication of certain statistical compendia and guides to statistical sources.

Doubtless the most extensive current arrangements are those that, for census use, provide access to the records of the Social Security Administration and the Internal Revenue Service. In the case of the former, the file of employers is maintained on a classified basis by means of the Standard Industrial Classification codes provided by the Census Bureau. The combination of information in the files of the Social Security Administration and the Internal Revenue Service provides the information needed for the Census Bureau to be able to mail the proper kind of reporting form to each business. In the case of multi-establishment firms, an additional canvass is made to get a list of the component establishments that should receive census forms. The conditions under which industry codes are supplied to the Social Security Administration by the Bureau were reviewed and approved by the Attorney General. With this information, the mailing list can be set up in such a way that each establishment will receive the appropriate form. The access to the Internal Revenue Service files is based upon an executive order giving Bureau employees access to the tax returns under specified conditions. As a result, the cost of the economic censuses has been substantially reduced, since information on the tax returns for small units makes it unnecessary to send census schedules to such firms.

Another example of cooperative arrangement with other agencies is embodied in the preparation of compendia and guides based upon information from a variety of agencies and published by the Government Printing Office. The best-known recurrent undertakings of this type are the long-established *Statistical Abstract of the United States,* issued annually, and closely related publications that are periodic supplements to the *Abstract.* These include the *Pocket Data Book, Historical Statistics of the United States, County and City Data Book,* and the *Congressional District Data Book.* Although the major part of these publications consists of data derived from the censuses and current surveys of the Bureau, many data from other sources are also included.

Another type of compendium, *Long Term Economic Growth,* consists of collections of time series directed to specific economic problems and issues. It provides a considerable body of annual series of economic statistics useful for the study of longer term trends.

In 1966 and 1967, the Bureau published two guides to federal statistics: *Directory of Federal Statistics for Local Areas* and *Directory of Federal Statistics for States.* In 1969, the Bureau issued a companion volume entitled *Directory of Non-Federal Statistics for States and Local Areas.*

Regulatory Agencies

From time to time, access to an individual census return is sought by a regulatory agency. The Bureau has always refused to accede to such requests, even though the agency may support its request with the argument that it has the power to obtain whatever information it needs through the power of subpoena. Accordingly, some agencies, notably the Federal Trade Commission, have sought to use the same form as that employed by the Census Bureau, with instructions to the company that the request could be met by supplying a copy of the return previously transmitted to the Bureau of the Census. The Bureau's objection to this approach is that it may be prejudicial to the interests of both the Bureau and the company to have another agency request, for regulatory purposes, estimates that had been prepared solely for statistical purposes. The consequence might be the withholding of future estimates from the Census Bureau and the loss of valuable statistical information on economic enterprises.

From the point of view of the Federal Trade Commission, a real break-through was achieved in the St. Regis case in December 1961, in which the Supreme Court held that the Federal Trade Commission could obtain from the St. Regis Paper Company its file copies of reports for the census of manufactures. The Census Bureau had, for many years, supplied companies with additional copies of the schedules, so that they might keep copies in their files to answer questions arising from the processing of the forms in Washington. Although the Bureau had believed that the information on such file copies was as safe from disclosure as the original return, the Supreme Court, in a 6-to-3 decision, found no specific guarantee of protection in the Census Law.

Evidence was soon forthcoming that the St. Regis decision would have adverse effects upon future cooperation with the Census Bureau. Early in 1962, therefore, bills were introduced to make immune from legal process respondents' file copies of confidential information that had been supplied to the Census Bureau. There was strong support for the new legislation from all but the regulatory agencies, and by October, 1962, remedial legislation had been passed by both houses of the Congress and signed by the President.

The Department of Justice

As a part of its legal functions, the Justice Department is occasionally called upon to ascertain the legality of proposed new procedures of the Census Bureau or to prosecute individuals or establishments failing to provide data required by law.

In addition to these functions, inherent in the Justice Department's role in government, there have been some special relationships in statistical areas related to crime.

In 1946, acting in close cooperation with the Office of Management and Budget (then the Bureau of the Budget), the Census Bureau announced discontinuance of a series of annual censuses of inmates of state and federal prisons and reformatories and a series regarding the disposition of defendants in criminal cases before the trial courts in thirty states. The latter series was open to a number of statistical shortcomings, and it was believed that the series would benefit from closer relationships with a Department having technical knowledge of the fields covered.

There followed a period of more than twenty years during which the Census Bureau output in the field of criminal statistics was limited to materials that were a by-product of the established censuses. In the latter part of the 1960's, however, the program-planning activities of the Census Bureau's Governments Division led to a series of meetings of experts in three areas: corrections, courts, and law enforcement. The consensus of these meetings was that there were great unmet needs for statistical information in fields related to crime, that a focal agency should be created, and that the Census Bureau should render any assistance possible through its specialized facilities for gathering and summarizing statistical data.

In accordance with these conclusions, the Census Bureau has worked on a number of projects at the request of the Law Enforcement Assistance Administration of the Justice Department. It has undertaken a criminal justice report, providing finance and employment data for all large governmental units and a sample of smaller units. Another project has involved a survey of public criminal justice agencies, in order to provide a directory of such agencies for use as a sampling framework for further research in this field. From the addresses located in the directory survey, a national survey was made of local jail facilities. An attack was also made on the feasibility of studies to measure the total impact of crime against individuals, businesses, and state and local governments. There is ample evidence that the total amount of victimization greatly exceeds that which appears in published reports on crime and that the problem of developing over-all measurement is one on which the Justice Department can make use of the facilities of the Census Bureau. On the basis of these recent developments, it would appear that the service relationships with the Justice Department may become somewhat similar to those in the public health field.

RELATIONSHIPS WITH STATE AND LOCAL GOVERNMENTS

State and local laws account for much of the interdependence of the Census Bureau and state and local agencies. Although some of the applications of census data to local needs are very widely known (for example, the distribution of many kinds of funds), a knowledge of the full extent of this dependence would require a careful study of state legislation. In one or two cases where this has been done, the pervasive influence of population size as a regulating device has been demonstrated by the fact that the form of local governments, the ability to borrow money and issue bonds, the numbers and type of officials, their salaries, granting of licenses of various types, and a host of other matters depend directly upon official counts from the latest population census. In one notable case, a county successfully used a special census as a basis for canceling the charter of a municipality that had been notorious as a center for gambling and prostitution and had thereby become obnoxious to the rest of the county. The county officials suspected that the municipality had been created by temporarily moving enough apparent residents into the area to provide a total in excess of fifty. A later special census taken without notice to the municipality in advance yielded a number below fifty and the municipality was dissolved, an action later upheld by the Supreme Court of the state.

Establishment of Official Boundaries

The Census Bureau is completely dependent upon local authorities for information about the legal status and latest boundaries of all minor civil divisions. Such information is essential for the proper allocation of all census returns to the area of residence. About two years before the date of a census, the Bureau undertakes the collection of up-to-date maps and information on all boundary changes since the last census. The subdivisions include: states, counties, or other subdivisions of states (such as parishes in Louisiana); townships, magisterial districts or other components of counties, cities, towns, villages, and boroughs; wards of cities, and congressional districts.

Detailed maps are needed for the more than 3,000 counties, for nearly 50,000 incorporated places and minor civil divisions, and for the heavily built up areas around cities of 50,000 and over. Special maps are needed also for the more than 3,000 unincorporated places delineated in advance of the census. The specifications for the maps are intended to provide completely up-to-date information regarding the boundaries of all places, as well as reports on incorporations and disincorporations. In addition, the local authorities are requested to keep the Bureau informed of any changes taking place up to the April 1 date set for each decennial census.

Redistricting

With the 1961 Supreme Court decision affirming the so-called "one man one vote" rule, the states have greater dependence than ever upon the Census Bureau for the detailed information necessary to subdivide their territory for legislative purposes. This applies, first of all, to the redistricting required in the states on the basis of the results of a new census. In this case, extremely fast action is required because of the established date for the sessions of the state legislatures in which the new boundaries must be approved.* Detailed census data are also required in connection with the new districts set up for the state legislatures. The data used for the creation of all the new subdivisions include population counts for the smallest political subdivisions, for city blocks, and for the enumeration districts used in taking the census. If the latter enumeration district figures are used, maps are also needed, so that boundaries can be established for legislative use.

Joint Efforts

For much of its history, the Census Bureau has had little contact with the statistical work of the states, even though a number of them have taken censuses of population and of industry. The last half of the 1960's, however, saw the beginning of an effort to bring about improved communication on statistical programs among federal, state, and local groups. The objectives of this effort were fourfold: (1) to identify the urgent needs for statistics; (2) to promote joint efforts toward common classifications and better data collection procedures; (3) to promote the interrelated use of federal and locally generated data; and (4) to make state and local officials, as well as other decision-makers better informed about federal statistics and their applicability to local uses. The foundations for the program were laid by the 1965 National Governors' Conference. As an outgrowth of this, there was a National Conference on Comparative Statistics in February, 1966, sponsored jointly by the Governors' Conference and the Council

---

* Following the 1970 election, the situation was acute in a few states where political shifts were to take place by the end of the year. Accordingly, they sought final data soon enough to permit the redistricting under the supervision of the Administration that would shortly be replaced. Charges of favoritism in the treatment of such requests were reviewed in congressional subcommittee hearings in December 1970.

of State Governments. In response to the needs and interest expressed at that conference, the Census Bureau established an Intergovernmental Services Program for state and local government officials. A major part of this program consists of a series of five-day seminars to focus on the kinds of information available from the Census Bureau and from other federal agencies. The first series of seminars was for officials from the states, the second for city representatives, and the third for city, county, and regional planning organizations, as well as for university research bureaus. Those in attendance from the federal system included the Office of Management and Budget (which worked with Census in planning the several series) and other federal statistical agencies. The discussions not only covered current programs but also plans for the future and some of the problems likely to be encountered in new undertakings.

Another type of joint effort with the states has been in the field of local population estimates. In 1967, the Bureau started a series of workshops with invited representatives from the states to study the techniques of making population estimates, the standardization of methodology for such work, and means of evaluating the results. Agreements to participate in this program have been made by the Bureau with forty-six of the fifty states, and special agencies of the state governments have been designated to work on the program. The continuation of this joint operation exemplifies the operation of a "creative federalism" under which guidance and assistance from the federal government can greatly benefit state operated programs, which in turn will strengthen the basis for many decisions at federal levels.

XI

The Census Bureau and Congress

In view of its periodic contacts with every household and most businesses in the country, the Census Bureau could scarcely avoid having frequent contacts with Congress. The most important of these in both houses are with standing subcommittees of the committees on Appropriations and of the committees on the Post Office and Civil Service. Annually, and more often when emergency needs arise, the Bureau's financial requirements are reviewed by subcommittees of the Appropriations committees of the House and Senate. The committees responsible for an overview of Census operations have less regular schedules for contact with the Bureau, but in the years immediately preceding a new decennial census, they may schedule two or three meetings in a single year. At times, Bureau representatives may be asked to comment on legislative proposals that involve the use of census data or require new data. Still other contacts take place with committees that are concerned with the constitutional rights of individuals and the possible invasion of privacy and, therefore, wish detailed information about the plans of the Bureau and the safeguards applied to its records.

Contacts with individual congressmen outside the committees are extremely numerous and quite varied. Members of Congress frequently make contacts in behalf of constituents who want jobs, promotions, or the withdrawal of adverse personnel actions. They also request data for the use of constituents or for their own needs. In some instances, where census results might damage a local area, congressmen may launch or support attacks on the statistics involved, particularly when local figures or estimates tell a different story. Still other contacts with congressmen flow out of their transmission of the complaints of citizens and businesses unwilling or unable to meet some of the data requirements of the Bureau.

APPROPRIATIONS

The regular appearances before the House and Senate appropriations subcommittees are undoubtedly the most crucial of all the congressional contacts required of Census and Departmental staffs. The outcome of these hearings determines whether the Bureau can undertake some or all of the new work that has been approved by the Department and the Office of Management and Budget. Ordinarily, adverse subcommittee actions are limited to the denial of some or all of the increases requested, and funds are usually granted to permit the continuation of all previously approved programs. In some cases, however, because of a change of administration, or other special circumstances, funds may be cut below the level of the preceding year, with the result that a reduction in force is required. Another factor adds to the importance of the testimonies of Census representatives—as a purely statistical agency, the Bureau has recurrently suffered from the lack of a powerful and continuing group of public sponsors with strong vested interests in its work. The publications of the Bureau are of value to a very wide range of business and government users, but there is no single group sufficiently concerned to make congressional representations, except when funds for a particular program have been cut off. In view of the stakes involved, it is not surprising that agency preparations for the appropriation hearings extend over a number of weeks, with intensive briefing sessions and preparation of quite detailed back-up material for dealing with unforeseen inquiries.

The seniority system, which determines the chairmanship of the subcommittees, is no guarantee of effectiveness. In some instances, the chairman acts merely as a presiding officer who makes no effort to evaluate individual programs and is completely dependent upon the clerk of the subcommittee. In other instances, the chairman comes to a hearing with a strong prejudice against all or part of the particular agency's work, perhaps because of his own background or because of a complaint registered by an important constituent.

During most of the years that the author of this volume appeared before the Appropriations Committee of the House (Subcommittee on Departments of State, Justice, and Commerce, and the Judiciary), Congressman John J. Rooney served as chairman. He was an extraordinarily capable and competent chairman, always ready to give careful consideration to new ideas. His dedication to economical management and efficient operations was perhaps unmatched in the Congress. My views, as Director of the Bureau, however, were not shared by all witnesses who came before Rooney. His vigor in challenging programs that he believes to be unwise or poorly administered has sometimes made him a target for attack. In 1968 he barely escaped being defeated in the primaries in his district, and his re-election in 1970 was by a smaller margin than usual.

Although apprehension was always the dominant emotion in hearings before Rooney, in retrospect, admiration for his workmanship leaves the strongest impression. After a brief exchange of courtesies and introduction of new people, he would always get to work with the efficiency developed from long experience and from extensive knowledge of all parts of the departmental mission. The record for each appropriation category was skillfully created by the chairman to include the supporting material presented by the agency, together with answers to questions asked by the chairman on his own initiative or suggested by his very able clerk, Jay Howe. The size of the hearing record was held to the minimum believed necessary for later use of the full committee or of Congress in final debate on the bill.

We were often uncertain whether the chairman had been favorably impressed by a particular presentation, but we were never in the dark when he was displeased. His impatience with any seeming evasion of the intent of his question or with an unduly long answer was well known to many of us from personal experience. On one occasion, after a long response on the importance of sampling, he reached into a drawer and brought out a set of articulated dentures, which he operated with sound effects to illustrate the wordiness of the proceeding response.

I believe that all of us who have appeared before congressional committees have had at least one horrible example of the hazards of an overlong reply. Such a reply can bring a challenge from committee members and thus damage the case presented by the agency, unless enough time is allowed to clarify the situation. Therefore it may be advisable to submit a reply for the record, even though material for a reasonably good immediate response is available in the files brought to the hearing. The advantage of a prompt reply is obvious, for it indicates that the witnesses have come well prepared.

An experienced and competent Appropriations chairman can be a source of strength in supporting innovations and can provide a stabilizing influence against unreasonable attacks and charges. Congressman Rooney deserved much credit for his willingness to support the development of electronic equipment for census use at a time when no one could guarantee the outcome. The task took longer than expected, and

Rooney asked many searching questions each year on the performance of the new equipment. In several hearings, he clearly indicated his disappointment over the length of the "shakedown" period, but he continued to support the funding of computers, even though costs rose sharply as UNIVAC I was succeeded by more sophisticated equipment.

On the other hand, the chairman's judgment regarding Bureau operations and needs can be an important element in enabling the Bureau to weather attacks that would otherwise be much more troublesome. One example of this was afforded by the claim of Sindlinger and Company, a market research firm, that funds should not be made available to the Bureau to continue a survey of consumer buying intentions previously financed by the Federal Reserve Board. Mr. Sindlinger had made his initial complaint to the conference committee of the House and Senate acting on 1962 appropriation requests, arguing that the investment made by his company in measuring consumer intentions would be jeopardized by giving a government agency funds that would enable it to work in the same field. Since there was too little time to review the merit of the Sindlinger case, the conference committee decided that the appropriation request should be deferred without prejudice until the following year.

In the months that followed, both the Council of Economic Advisers and the Federal Reserve Board indicated their support of the Census request, and support was also given by the Federal Statistics Users' Conference, which appointed a special committee of nongovernment people to look into the issue. Nevertheless, Sindlinger renewed his complaint the next year and the issue was examined by the subcommittee under the chairmanship of Congressman John J. Rooney. An opportunity was afforded in the hearing to bring out the government's strong interest in subjecting this kind of research to close review at all times and to show that government interests cannot be subordinated to those of a private organization.

A further point of considerable importance was that the Census Bureau would be simply continuing work that it had performed for three years with Federal Reserve funds, an activity that had not been opposed by Sindlinger. Although the funds requested were approved in the House, the Senate committee was apparently more impressed by the Sindlinger arguments and denied the money. The funds were finally made available by the action of the conference committee in which the views of the House prevailed. In retrospect, it is apparent that it would have been easy for a less thorough or courageous chairman to conclude that the government could get along on the basis of measures of consumer plans provided by private marketing organizations.

Another example of Rooney's stabilizing influence came in the course of the controversy over the conduct of the 1970 census. His Subcommittee on State, Justice, Commerce, and the Judiciary and later the full Congress had supported the experimental work needed to carry out much of the 1970 census by mail and had also been informed of shortcomings in the 1960 census coverage, which could be reduced only by the expenditure of considerably larger sums of money in taking the census. At the hearings on funds for 1969, Rooney asked questions to bring out the relatively small difference between the content of the 1960 and 1970 censuses, the effect of a reduction in the funds allowed by the Congress, and the advisability of having many of the census questions postponed for inclusion in a sample household survey to be undertaken in a later year. After this series of questions, he pointedly asked the Director of the Census how long he had been with the Bureau of the Census (twenty-nine years). After all of this he introduced into the record a letter which he had received from Congressman Jackson Betts, suggesting that the census would benefit from a substantial reduction in the content of the schedules and a postponement of some of the inquiries to later surveys. Betts further suggested that the savings from reduction of the 1970 operation would be sufficient to pay for the sample surveys for one or more later years. Rooney requested that the Director supply the subcommittee with a detailed response to each of the points contained in the letter from Betts. To those who had become "Rooney-watchers" over the years, it seemed most significant that the chairman had given the principal witness a chance to testify regarding the length of his census service and to refute the letter before it was put into the record. It was no surprise, therefore, that the House report on the 1969 funds contained no reference to the Betts proposal, and the amounts requested for the 1970 census were approved in full.

The role of the corresponding Senate appropriations sub-committee (on State, Justice, Commerce, and the Judiciary) is normally limited to a review of those parts of the House report that the Bureau wishes to appeal. During recent years, the Senate subcommittee has been headed by Senator John L. McClellan of Arkansas, who has shown little interest in statistical work. Under these circumstances, it has usually seemed wisest to accept the action of the House rather than to appeal to the Senate and run the risk of further reductions.

In some cases, however, when the Office of Management and Budget and other agencies do feel that an appeal is essential because of the great urgency of a program, an appeal is made to the Senate subcommittee. For example, in the requests for 1968, the House had disapproved a $20 million request to conduct a household survey to update some of the 1960 information for states and large cities. The appeal to the Senate was for $11.5 million to carry out a somewhat reduced survey. Most of the discussion turned upon the chairman's interest in having the survey identify families with irregular living arrangements and illegitimate children. The Director of the Bureau was sure that he had not convinced McClellan that this would require questions inappropriate for a census survey, and near the end of the hearing Senator Mc-

Clellan said, "I can say for one member of this committee you have not made much of a case as far as I am concerned, sir." As had been anticipated from the outset, the appeal was turned down.

OVER-ALL PROGRAM REVIEW

From the time of the first census, the Bureau has been subject to surveillance by congressional committees, first by a series of *ad hoc* committees and then by a standing committee. Prior to the establishment of the permanent bureau in 1902, and indeed until 1929, legislation was usually enacted each decade to provide for the forthcoming decennial census (except for the years 1800–30), and there was also separate legislation to effect the new apportionment of seats in the House.

With the creation of the permanent bureau in 1902, there was for the first time a need for a standing committee. The House Census Committee was created in 1901 and continued to function until the Legislative Reorganization Act of 1946. During this period, landmark acts were enacted with regard both to basic census law and apportionment, and the program of basic censuses was considerably modified by the addition of new inquiries and by increasing the frequency of some censuses. The 1929 Act was the first to give the Director authority to determine the content of the census and also the first in eighty years to include provision for reapportionment. A little over ten years later, the committee closely examined the question of apportionment. The resulting legislation made reapportionment after each census automatic unless Congress should take action to the contrary and, as noted in Chapter II, prescribed the use of the method of equal proportions, which has been used for every subsequent census.

In 1946, legislative oversight of Census programs was assigned to the committees on the Post Office and Civil Service in the House and Senate. The decision to assign Census to these committees rather than to those oriented to other parts of the Commerce Department doubtless reflected the fact that the Census Bureau, like the Post Office Department and the Civil Service Commission, has a government-wide mission. In any case, the decision was a particularly happy one in view of the developments in the 1960's when the Census Bureau was to have extremely close relations with the Post Office Department in working out plans to take most of the 1970 census by mail. One further change in committee arrangements took place at the beginning of the Eighty-sixth Congress in 1959, when a Subcommittee on Census and Government Statistics (later to be shortened to Census and Statistics) was set up in the House to make a broad continuing study of collection, publication, and use of all government statistics. In the 1960's, the Census Bureau accounted for a large part of the work load of the new subcommittee. Two of its first hearings covered the plans and some personnel aspects of the 1960 census. Unfortunately, this review was held too close to April 1, 1960, to give the subcommittee much opportunity to influence the planning.

The subcommittee's first entry into a new field of statistics involved a review in 1961 of the methods of reducing reporting requirements in transportation. Much of the testimony in the hearings provided the basis for a favorable report on a census of transportation, which had never been taken, even though provided for in legislation since 1948. It is quite likely that the encouragement thus given to this particular census was an important element accounting for the 1963 Census of Transportation, the first in this series.

Census by Mail

The Subcommittee on Census and Statistics considered the modification of existing legislation to assure the Census Bureau of the legality of its plans to collect much of the 1970 census by mail. The minimum need in this connection was to remove the apparent requirement that enumerators visit every household in order to take the census. Consideration of the appropriate legislation extended over three calendar years, the delay arising mainly from differences of opinion as to how much change should be made in the provisions for duties of enumerators, supervisors, and other census personnel. The Bureau's original proposal had been that legislation on these subjects be repealed and the necessary control be achieved by Bureau regulation. The Senate committee was not in agreement, however, and the outcome was a bill that modified the statute only to the extent necessary to permit the census-by-mail approach. A separate revision of the law, approved at the same time, made it possible for the first time to reimburse enumerators for telephone calls made in connection with getting information from households.

Mid-Decade Census

The subcommittee has given a good deal of time to the drafting and reviewing of legislative proposals that there be a mid-decade census in 1965 or later. A number of bills along this line were introduced annually, beginning in 1961, and extensive hearings took place in 1961, 1965, and 1967. In the last years of this series, when a 1965 census was out of the question, the target date was shifted to 1967 or 1968, or to a series beginning in 1975. Most of the testimony at all of the hearings was highly favorable, but Administration approval of the bills was withheld because the Office of Management and Budget believed that a better use of the needed funds would be to expand programs for sample surveys and population estimates. In 1967, however, the wording of the bill was modified to state that the census for 1975 and every ten years thereafter "make maximum use of sampling procedures consistent with statistical needs." Viewing this as assurance that a 1975 census would not become a duplication of the 1970 operation, the Office of Management and Budget gave administration support for the new measure. With some minor amendments, the bill was reported favorably by the full Committee on the Post Office and Civil Service and was passed in the House by a 255 to 127 vote in August 1967. But hearings in the Senate did not take place until the following year, and the bill was never reported out of the Senate Committee. (The reason most frequently given on an unofficial basis was that Senator Mike Monroney feared that it might have an adverse effect on his campaign for re-election. He was not re-elected). The 2-to-1 margin in the House was the high-water mark of the latest campaign for a mid-decade census. Public support for a mid-decade census has remained strong, and the subject seems likely to receive much attention in the next few years.

The 1970 Census

The first review of plans for the 1970 census took place in August, 1966, a date early enough to ensure that the views of committee members could have substantial impact. It is probable that neither the staff of the Bureau nor that of the subcommittee realized that some of the issues brought out in this hearing were to serve as the forerunners of a major controversy. The first witness was Congressman Cornelius E. Gallagher of New Jersey, who, as chairman of the Special Subcommittee on Invasion of Privacy of the House Committee on Government Operations, had recently become concerned over a proposed national data bank. Gallagher commended the Census Bureau on its plan to take much of the 1970 census by mail and on other evidence of its concern about protecting privacy. The congressman was opposed, however, to questions on religious preference and social security number and expressed much concern over the possibility of having any federal data placed in a national data bank. He felt that such a plan would bring about dangers of disclosure much greater than those existing under the current system in which data are dispersed among a number of agencies.

A second set of hearings on the 1970 census took place in May and June, 1967, when Deputy Postmaster General Frederick C. Belen appeared and told about the joint tests that had been conducted to determine the capability of the Post Office Department to perform the work required to take the 1970 census by mail. At the same hearings, there was extensive discussion of most of the questions proposed for the census and the reasons for their inclusion. The interest of the Subcommittee on Census and Statistics in the new procedures for 1970 led to a considerable number of inquiries regarding the recent New Haven census test, the areas to be covered on a mail basis, the source of the mailing lists, and the procedures to be followed in cases of families that do not send back their forms. Comparative costs and alternative arrangements were the subject of a number of the inquiries from subcommittee members. One or two appeared to be surprised that the Census had gone as far as it had in making commitments to the new plans without having had specific approval from the subcommittee. As a matter of fact, the plans for the new approach had been clearly stated in the hearings of the previous year, and the steps for executing them were clearly matters of administration rather than policy. One further development in the hearings during the spring of 1967 was the appearance of Congressman Jackson E. Betts to give information about his bill to make census responses voluntary, except for seven questions.

Hearings in October 1967 on the Betts Bill, H.R. 10952, were essentially a concession to Betts in return for his support on the mid-decade census bill. In Betts' appearance before the subcommittee, he particularly stressed the ability of market research organizations to get information from households without the benefit of any compulsory authority. Opposition to his bill appeared in the testimony of Congressman

Gallagher, in a statement in behalf of the Federal Statistics Users' Conference, and in letters from many state and local organizations.

Although there was much discussion of the limiting legislation throughout 1968, both in the Congress and outside, there were no further hearings until April and May, 1969. On the basis of these hearings as a whole, the subcommittee, and especially its new chairman, Congressman Charles H. Wilson of California, became convinced that the Betts Bill was unwise but that a more moderate form of remedial legislation would be useful. Such legislation, despite opposition by the Administration, passed the House but was not brought up for formal consideration in the Senate. Nevertheless, the House Committee on the Post Office and Civil Service had been successful in completing its work prior to 1970, when further legislative discussion could have been especially damaging, and in the process, many of the members had acquired a great deal of familiarity with the issues and with Census procedures and standards.

OTHER CONGRESSIONAL COMMITTEES

From time to time, representatives of the Census Bureau are called upon to appear before various committees, often in connection with proposed legislation or with the applicability of census data to a certain kind of problem. In such hearings, Census officials serve in a purely technical capacity, without any recommendation as to policy.

Voting Rights

A particularly interesting set of hearings were those held in the spring of 1965 on the Voting Rights Act of 1965. Under this proposed legislation, in states and political subdivisions of states determined by the Attorney General, the Director of the Census was to determine whether "less than 50 percentum of the persons of voting age residing therein were registered on November 1, 1964, or that less than 50 percentum of such persons voted in the presidential election of November 1964." In the Judiciary committees of both the House and the Senate, much time was spent in considering the work the Census Bureau would do in meeting the requirements of the law and the time and cost involved. The interpretation of the phrase "political subdivision" was an issue of some importance, since it would have material effect upon the cost of compliance by the Bureau. Census estimates could be provided at quite reasonable cost for states and counties, but the provision of similar figures for subdivisions of counties would ordinarily require special surveys or censuses.

Senator Sam J. Ervin, Jr., an extraordinarily able constitutional lawyer, who was acting as chairman of the hearing, was obviously unhappy over the legislation. He spent a great deal of time developing the point that the Census Bureau could not provide figures for that part of the formula referring to the relationship between the total population and those registered to vote. In about twenty exchanges between Senator Ervin and the writer (then Acting Director of the Census), the senator emphasized the lack of systematic data on registration, while the Acting Director endeavored to indicate that lack of information on the percentage registered is not important, since the percentage voting will always be less than the percentage registered. Finally, in a most welcome intervention, Senator Everett Dirksen in his rolling prose stated, "Mr. Eckler, standing in Section 3(a) as big as the moon on Rockaway Beach, is the word 'or' ". After the completion of extensive hearings and congressional debate, the Voting Rights Act was finally approved in August 1965, and within a few months the Census Bureau had carried out its duties as specified by the Attorney General. Unfortunately, the Bureau's image was temporarily tarnished in the South, where its findings in some cases led to voting registration programs under federal auspices.

Apportionment and Redistricting

In the first 150 years of the nation's history, Congress brought a number of variations into the method used for the apportionment of seats among the states. In some cases, the number of seats was increased at the time of the new apportionment, with the result that there were no losses for any state and gains for a great many. Even after the 1940 census, when apportionment became automatic after the census and when a single method was prescribed, little attention was given to the manner in which the states took account of the new figures. In recent years, however, Congress has become increasingly concerned with the great disparities in size among congressional districts and has considered various proposals to make them more nearly uniform. In the famous *Baker* v. *Carr* decision in 1962, the Supreme Court judicially recognized the Constitutional right of a citizen to have his vote count equally with that of other citizens of the state and asserted the role of the federal judiciary in assuring this right. This gave strong impetus to congressional efforts to prescribe standards for establishment of districts within the states. Evidence of the new interest was provided by the fact that in the hearings on the 1970 census, three different subcommittees * raised questions concerning the treatment of the U.S. population overseas and suggested that it should be added to the resident population of each state for the purpose of determining congressional representation. In response to this, the Census Bureau developed a plan for obtaining information on persons in the armed forces and government civilian employees and their dependents overseas, including data on their home states. This plan, after approval by the Attorney General and clearance with the House Judiciary Committee, was followed in the preparation

* The Constitutional Rights Subcommittee of the Senate Committee on the Judiciary, the Subcommittee on Economic Statistics of the Joint Economic Committee, and the Subcommittee on Census and Statistics of the House Committee on Post Office and Civil Service.

of the report to the President made at the end of November, 1970.

Privacy and Confidentiality

In the last half of the 1960's, the Census Bureau had contacts with a number of committees on various aspects of the relationship of the census to the rights of individuals. The first of these took place in June 1965 before a subcommittee of the House Committee on Government Operations under the direction of Congressman Cornelius Gallagher. The subcommittee indicated concern over the possibilities of invasion of privacy of members of the household of a farm operator when they are asked to furnish income information through the operator. A satisfactory alternative was agreed upon: for future censuses of agriculture, individuals were given the option of sending in their returns by mail. In 1967, the subcommittee on Administrative Practice and Procedure of the Senate Judiciary Committee held hearings on issues connected with the possible establishment of a National Data Center. The census testimony was largely concerned with the provisions used to ensure confidentiality of census data.

Two more hearings in the same broad area took place in 1969 in connection with the legislation proposed by Congressman Betts to reduce the amount of mandatory authority applying to census questions. The first of these was before Senator Ervin, chairman of the Constitutional Rights Subcommittee of the Senate Committee on the Judiciary. The hearings were on the subject of legislation that Ervin had introduced to limit both the kinds of questions to be asked of individuals by government agencies and the authority for compelling or requesting cooperation. The other hearing, before the Subcommittee on Economic Statistics of the Joint Economic Committee, was designed to help the Administration in the battle against repressive census legislation by introducing a number of witnesses able to testify regarding the great importance of the forthcoming census and the damage to the results if responses to most questions were made voluntary.

Application to Legislative Problems

From time to time, representatives of the Census Bureau are called upon for special tabulations or testimony about the applicability of census figures to a particular purpose. Thus, for antitrust work in the Senate, the Census Bureau has prepared special tabulations to show the amount of concentration in various segments of industry. It has done this by a tabulation of the proportion of shipments in each industry accounted for by the four largest and eight largest companies. Another example was provided by hearings in 1965 before a subcommittee of the House Committee on Education and Labor, which was devoted to ascertaining the availability of family income data needed for the distribution of funds to strengthen and improve educational quality in the nation's elementary and secondary schools. On two different occasions in 1969, an associate director of the Bureau was asked to testify before the House Committee on Banking and Currency regarding recent population changes as revealed by various social and economic measures.

RELATIONS WITH INDIVIDUAL CONGRESSMEN

In both the House and the Senate, population is a factor in determining the money available for staff assistance. In the case of the House, the magic figure is 500,000 for a district, and the Census Bureau is continuously in touch with all available evidence to determine if and when a district near that level has in fact exceeded it. Disagreements between Census officials and local representatives of chambers of commerce and universities are not infrequent, but on the whole congressmen have accepted the census figures even when they have been disappointed. In the Senate, there are a number of population levels, starting at 3 million and going as high as 17 million, which determine the amount of staff assistance allowed for individual senators. Controversies here are less frequent since the Bureau's long-standing estimates of the population of states have been quite widely accepted.

Under the provisions of the Census Law, all field appointments for the decennial census are made without regard to the Classification Act, but tests have been applied to all candidates for such positions. Usually candidates for the positions of managers of the district offices for each census (some four hundred) are nominated by Administration members of Congress, or in some cases by alternative sources designated by the Administration. The candidates are interviewed and tested by the permanent staff of the Bureau and are appointed only if they are found suitable for the task. The district managers and the permanent regional staffs are then responsible for the recruiting of their local staffs, working through referral sources that have been approved by a congressional or national source.

There is some evidence that congressmen and senators may lose interest in having the traditional system continued. The use of rigorous tests and the need to reject many unsuitable candidates may bring embarrassment to the members of Congress responsible for the original recommendation. Hence, some members have reached the view that they would be better off if they had no responsibilities for nominating candidates for Census jobs. Their views are represented in the words of Congressman H. R. Gross in the August 1966 hearings on 1970 Census Questions: "I wish the day would come in this country when we could select enumerators, rural mail carriers, and postmasters on something other than a political basis, and I have been on both sides of the fence. I hope the day will come when people performing these services will be free from politics."

XII

The Census Bureau and the Public

The Census Bureau is the only government agency required to make periodic contact with every household in the United States. Some might think the Postal Service shares this responsibility, but there are significant numbers who receive no mail and have had no contact with any part of the Postal Service. The Social Security Administration and Internal Revenue Service have huge "publics," but many households have never been reached by either agency.

The Census Bureau is the only statistical agency of the government with mandatory authority for the collection of data from individuals and establishments. Enacted at the time of the first population census, this mandatory authority now applies to all the periodic censuses, except the census of governments. The exception is due to lack of federal authority over state and local governments. Reports can also be required in the case of sample surveys conducted no more frequently than once a year. Such a report may be made mandatory if restricted to inquiries of the kind included in the periodic censuses, and if advance notice is given to respondents by announcement published in the *Federal Register*. Reports of data collected more than once a year are on a voluntary basis, except for those authorized by special legislation governing series of strategic importance.

CONFIDENTIALITY OF RETURNS

Most people who are familiar with the present strong provisions for the protection of information obtained from the public take it for granted that this protection has always been associated with the power to compel response. It seems natural to assume that anyone required to fill out census forms regarding himself or his activities should be assured that the information would be safeguarded by the Bureau. As a matter of fact, for much of its long history, the Census Bureau did its work without any legislative provision to ensure the confidential treatment of individual returns. The transition to the present system of full protection was a gradual one, involving several stages.

In the first five censuses (1790–1830), copies of the returns were posted in two public places, so that additions could be made for missing households or missing members. While it is true that the information given to the census taker was relatively simple, many persons today would be offended at having information of this kind posted in a public place. The lack of any protection in the early years probably reflects the fact that our census, like those of other countries, owed its origin to the needs of government, whether for the military, the raising of taxes, or apportioning the number of representatives for use by each state. In line with the emphasis upon government needs, copies of the returns for the early years were deposited with the local courts.

For the 1840 census, the authorizing act required the Secretary of State to transmit to the marshals "regulations and instructions pursuant to this act." The instructions to the assistant marshals (the enumerators) contained the following sentence: "It is, moreover, inculcated upon the assistant that he consider all communications made to him in the performance of his duty, relative to the business of the people, as strictly confidential."

Two reasons can be surmised for the restrictions on enumerators. First, there had been a notable increase in the amount of economic data collected, so that the administrators might have deemed it wise to limit the enumerators in the use of such information. Second, the regulations may have been introduced in the hope of getting more reliable answers from the public. There is reason to believe that the interest of a statistical agency in getting both complete and reliable answers from respondents would in time lead it to adopt strict confidentiality provisions regardless of any law to compel such action. Indeed, the chief value of such statutes is the assurance they give of continuity. Returns were still posted publicly in 1840, so the restrictions upon enumerators were apparently limited to the treatment of information beyond that recorded on the census forms. With the discontinuance of public posting in 1850, the regulations applying to the field organization became a more significant safeguard, but there was still no restriction of any kind upon Census staff not concerned with data collection.

The 1880 census, the first to be carried out under the Department of the Interior rather than by federal marshals, was taken under a law that included an oath of nondisclosure for field workers and a penalty for violation. Information filed with the local courts was limited to "a list of the names, with age, sex, and color, of all persons enumerated." Such information was available on a fee basis, at the specific request of the municipal government. Inasmuch as the law placed no restriction upon personnel outside the field organization, the records of the 1880 and 1890 censuses (the latter largely destroyed by fire) as well as those of all earlier censuses, have been made available to the public in the National Archives.

With the Act providing for the 1900 census, confidential treatment of the census records was, for the first time, required of all employees, and penalties for violation were applicable to everyone. Thus, the records for the 1900 and later censuses have not been made available for public use, despite recurrent demands from historians and genealogists for access to (at least) the 1900 files on the grounds that the passage of time has removed any danger of detriment to individuals. The possibility of injury to descendants might conceivably exist for a great many years, but the release of such records for public use a hundred years later would probably arouse little criticism from even the strictest advocates of confidentiality.

Although the protection accorded by the 1900 law was rather comprehensive, some later developments have significantly tightened the original provisions. In the law for the 1910 census, attention was given for the first time to the possibility of disclosure through published reports. Publication was to be made in a form that would not reveal the report of any establishment. The danger of disclosure is particularly great in the industrial censuses, where a single large unit may dominate the total for a small area. The danger is much less in the case of the population and agriculture censuses, which were not given similar legal protection until 1930.

Another feature of the gradual tightening of the confidentiality provisions has been the narrowing of the transfer authority given to the Director of the Census. In the 1900 and 1910 censuses, the Director was to furnish names, age, sex, color, and place of birth at the request of governors and courts of record upon the payment of the cost involved. In 1920, this was sharply limited by the provision that in no case should information thus furnished be used to the detriment of the person to whom it relates. Evidently, this limitation did not immediately cut off all such work, for in the 1923 report of the Secretary of Commerce, reference is made to the supplying of names and addresses of illiterates to a number of states. Nevertheless, as a matter of practice, the detriment restriction is a substantial roadblock in the way of any release, since there is a conceivable detriment in almost every case. Thus, in the case of giving out the names and addresses of illiterates, it is quite possible that the release of this information would have been embarrassing and harmful to some of those so identified.

The lack of recent changes in the confidentiality laws and the unblemished record of the Census Bureau in maintaining the confidentiality of all records currently entrusted to it do not necessarily preclude the possibility that some revision of the law would be desirable. Neither does the fact that U.S. provisions are generally in line with those in effect in foreign countries. One proposed change, which was a part of a bill approved by the House in 1969 but not acted upon by the Senate, increased the penalties in order to emphasize the importance of strict compliance. Another possible change might be to reduce the degree of discretion exercised by the Director in the release of information for genealogical and other proper purposes.

Still another change that would appeal to some critics is legislation to destroy the names of all respondents on census returns so that it would be impossible to associate the name of an individual with any of the characteristics reported for him. This would involve the sacrifice of some uses that can be made of census results. Careful study is needed to determine whether the dangers involved in retention of names are substantial enough to justify the losses arising from their elimination.

APPLICATION OF CONFIDENTIALITY RULES

The attention given to the assurance of confidentiality under present laws can best be demonstrated by presenting a few examples covering legal decisions, the treatment of various kinds of requests, and the adoption of meticulous rules to avoid disclosure in published reports.

Legal Decisions

A landmark opinion of the Attorney General in 1930 provided the precedent for refusing requests from other federal agencies for information about individuals. At that time, shortly after the taking of the census, the Women's Bureau had requested a list of names, addresses, occupations, and employment status of women in Rochester, New York. The Census Bureau referred this to the Attorney General, who ruled against release of the information. In light of this decision, the earlier release of names and addresses of illiterates was clearly improper.

About thirty years later, the Bureau of the Census sought assurance regarding the protection of information collected by means of voluntary surveys. A 1962 opinion of the Attorney General stated that data collected by the Census Bureau on a voluntary basis are as fully protected from disclosure as those for which responses are required.

On the basis of the precedent set by the 1930 decision, the Census Bureau has turned down requests even under what might seem exceptional circumstances. Early in World War II, there was a program to relocate Japanese living in the West Coast states. The 1940 census listing would have been most useful in helping to locate persons of Japanese origin, but the Census Bureau did not provide such a list, and the task had to be done by other means. Another case of a quite different nature involved a request for data from farm schedules in the state of Washington in order to show damage from a smelter operation across the Canadian border in Trail, British Columbia. Although the international tribunal concerned with settling this damage suit believed that it could demand the census records under the terms of an international convention, it respected the action of the Census Bureau in declining to furnish the schedules. Still another case arose when the White House was being completely restored, and it was necessary to find a temporary residence for the President. At that time the Census Bureau turned down a request for information on persons living in an exclusive Washington subdivision.

Restrictions on Providing Personal Records

Despite the power of discretion given the Director of the Census to release personal data for genealogical and other proper purposes, the authority has seldom been used because of the necessity of avoiding detriment to individuals. Fortunately, most requests for personal information are perfectly clear-cut and justifiable. Millions of individuals who have no other means of proof of their ages can and have made use of the census records to establish their age, citizenship, or relationship to other members of the household and thus prove their eligibility for Social Security benefits, for Medicare, for issuance of passports, and for other purposes. Information of this sort is provided only to the person himself, to an agency he designates, or to his legally determined representative.

Mixed in with run-of-the-mill requests, granted whenever the information can be located in the records, are a considerable number that must be turned down, even though many of them promise to confer benefits upon the individual if he can be located. It is not proper, for example, to give any information to help a lawyer locate a missing heir, since the missing person may wish not to be located and would regard it as detrimental if the Census Bureau provided information that helped to find him. It is even more obvious why the Bureau cannot assist law enforcement and the taxing agencies in locating gamblers, racketeers, and tax delinquents.

Protection Against Disclosure by Publication

A great deal of careful analysis goes into the preparation of statistical tables that are published to ensure that no accidental disclosure of the information pertaining to an individual or an establishment occurs. In large areas, this is ordinarily not a problem, but in smaller areas a great deal of work is needed to ensure that tables based upon a small number of units may not lend themselves to inferential disclosure about an individual establishment. The operating rules have to take into account the fact that the presence of one or two very large establishments may lead to disclosure even though there are a considerable number of smaller units in the same area. There is also the danger of indirect disclosure by the publication of figures for two overlapping minor civil divisions, such as a city and the county in which it is located, one of them being only slightly larger than the other. In this case, the publication of certain kinds of industrial data for each of the two areas might make disclosure possible, since the difference between the two might include only one large plant located outside the city but within the county. A somewhat analogous type of disclosure would take place if the Bureau were to publish in separate tables information on the characteristics of the four largest and the six largest enterprises in a particular industry. By subtraction, totals could be obtained for firms in the fifth and sixth places that might enable each of them to determine the size of the other.

CENSUS INQUIRIES AND INDIVIDUAL PRIVACY

Regardless of the importance of census statistics for governmental and private decision-making and regardless of the rigorous protection accorded all information collected, there are some who feel that their privacy is violated whenever they are asked for information about themselves and their dwellings. The *U.S.* v. *Moriarity* case 70 years ago would seem to have established the right of a sovereign government to collect data. Nevertheless, the issue of privacy, among others, was involved in the case of the *United States* v. *Rickenbacker* (1962), in which one of the arguments was that the household questionnaire used in the 1960 census was unreasonable and hence in violation of the Fourth Amendment, which protects against "unreasonable searches and seizures." The District Court reached a decision in favor of the government and, upon appeal, the Second Court of Appeals upheld this action with the following statement: "The authority to gather reliable statistical data reasonably related to governmental purposes and functions is a necessity if modern government is to legislate intelligently and effectively." This was the final judgment in the case, since the Supreme Court declined to review it.

Some students of social trends argue that the increasing complexity of modern life and the pressures of an urban environment have increased the proportion of the population concerned about the census and other inquiries as an invasion of one of the areas of privacy still available to them. At any rate, the issue did not come to an end with the decision in the Rickenbacker case. The last half of the 1960's saw a strong increase in the amount of discussion of the various ways in which modern technology may intrude upon individual and family privacy. Some of those participating in these discussions have expressed the view that it would be better to accept some loss of efficiency in government, if that is the cost of guarding the privacy of the individual. It seems likely that the delicate art of balancing the government's need to know as a basis for governing will continue to be weighed against the individual's right to privacy, even though judicial and administrative actions over many years give full assurance of scrupulous handling of all census records.

PUBLIC AWARENESS OF THE CENSUS

The decennial population and housing census is such a massive undertaking that extensive communication with the public is required over a period of at least six years. There is first of all a long period when the public needs are being appraised so that the content of the schedules and the nature of the output can be planned intelligently. Second, the public must be informed about the data it will be called upon to supply, the need for the information, and the procedures being used. Third, as the results become available, a much smaller segment of the public needs to know about available data and services.

In preparation for the 1970 census, efforts were made to get suggestions from as many kinds of users as possible, but only a very small fraction of users actually had direct contact with Bureau officials. In 1966 and 1967, under the sponsorship of local chapters or members of professional associations, public meetings were held in twenty-three cities across the country. Representatives of state and local governments and of planning agencies were especially numerous in the various meetings, but the attendance was drawn also from business, research organizations, and the academic community. Since there was much similarity from city to city in the data needs expressed, it was concluded that additional coverage of areas would not yield any significant amount of new information.

Another device for eliciting public needs was a Council of Population and Housing Census Users, including representatives of the large professional associations in the social sciences, labor organizations, trade associations, and a variety of organizations concerned with housing, education, health, welfare, and urban matters generally. Since many of the representatives had canvassed their organizations in advance, the meetings of the council were especially productive.

Advisory committees, especially those representing professional associations, have undoubtedly been one of the most important sources of guidance concerning needs to be met by the periodic decennial censuses. The committees are particularly useful in giving an outside viewpoint on the records normally maintained by respondents that would provide the information necessary for answering census questions and on the willingness of respondents to cooperate. Because of the variety of the organizations from which they are drawn, they can often help in interpreting the purposes to be served by the various inquiries and thus bring about a higher degree of public cooperation. Doubtless the most influential advisory committee has been the Census Advisory Committee of the American Statistical Association, which is not only the oldest advisory committee serving the Bureau but is also the oldest existing committee of the association. In each of the semiannual meetings for several years in advance of the decennial census, substantial attention is given to the plans for the forthcoming census, including content, tabulation plans, and publications.

Committees of two other associations, the American Economic Association and the American Marketing Association, also give consideration to the plans for each decennial census. These committees meet once each year, and their major attention is devoted to the economic programs of the Bureau.

Still other advisory committees are concerned with one subject area, or with some particular aspects of the census. Thus, three *ad hoc* committees were organized for the most recent censuses of population, housing, and agriculture, to deal with questions of content, public relations, and output. As representatives of various classes of users, the committee members were able to sharpen judgments on the relative priority of items competing for inclusion in the census and their views regarding the character of the output helped the Bureau use its resources in the most effective manner. While the members were not selected to represent the suppliers of the information, their wide experience helped evaluate the probable public reaction to new inquiries or modification of old ones. Another group with a special function is the Advisory Committee on Small Area Data, which, as already noted, focuses its attention upon data needed for small areas for planning and administrative purposes.

Publicity

It has always proved advantageous to have the public as well informed as possible regarding the questions to be asked, the reasons for cooperation, and the procedures to be followed. The gains in time in the case of an enumerative census can be easily shown. If advance publicity can save half a minute of explanation for the enumerator, the total saving would be more than $1 million.

There were two reasons for an unusually careful program of public information about the 1970 census. First, the use of the mails for the initial collection of data for some 60 per cent of the nation's households placed a heavy premium upon efforts to get every household to cooperate by filling in the forms and mailing them to the local offices as soon as possible. Second, the increased tension in the central areas of most large cities called for unusual efforts to communicate with the various minority groups concentrated in these areas. Thus, the information program was two-pronged, one part directed to the general public, and the other to the special classes to be found in the inner-city areas.

All of the media helped inform the public of the significance of the forthcoming census. Some articles were published in 1969 and even earlier, serving to provide a general awareness of the 1970 census without getting into detail regarding plans and procedures. The great bulk of the materials, however, was targeted on the April 1, 1970 date, including the weeks immediately preceding and following. A series of feature stories for dailies and weeklies, supplemented by many special materials released through the field offices, provided massive, widely distributed newspaper coverage. Special stories by syndicated columnists were helpful in reaching many readers. Even the syndicated cartoonists were enlisted in the campaign, one notable example being the Steve Canyon series, where the taking of the census in a wilderness region was the theme of an eight-week segment. The periodicals that carried stories on the census covered a broad spectrum of readership, including labor, educators, health officials, veterans, women's organizations, business, and government.

Both television and radio were important factors in getting information to the public. Over 700 television stations and some 4,500 radio stations were provided with short filmed or recorded spots, together with live announcements and fact sheets. The spots were used extensively, with reports from the networks indicating a total of some 760 million impressions. Two five-minute films produced in cooperation with the Sperry Rand Corporation were widely distributed to promote individual understanding and cooperation. The television and radio programs were greatly assisted by the cooperation of celebrities in the field of entertainment, including a number who cooperated in producing spots for distribution to Spanish language stations and others in areas with considerable numbers of Spanish Americans.

In an effort to reach black audiences, scripts and special short announcements were distributed to "soul" stations and individual disc jockeys. In March, 1970, about 150 selected stations were provided with a recording of census messages by prominent black personalities. Government officials at all levels took part in informing the public of the forthcoming census. Particularly important was a two-minute talk taped by President Nixon for use by the radio networks on the morning of March 30. Top officials of the Commerce Department and the Census Bureau appeared on a variety of programs aimed at both national and regional audiences, as well as on local news and discussion programs.

In 1970, as in earlier censuses, the work done by the Advertising Council, Inc., was a powerful factor in broadening and strengthening the whole public information program. When the council approves a federal program for direct assistance, it brings to bear on the problem the volunteer professional services of a large advertising agency selected for that particular campaign. It is, moreover, equipped with the experience and contacts necessary to obtain advertising coverage in newspapers and magazines, as well as on radio and television. Through the efforts of the council, a series of advertisements were run by weekly and daily newspapers, some for a full series of thirteen weeks and others for shorter periods. The total lineage represented by these advertisements was nearly 2 million. In addition, advertisements appeared in general magazines and business publications with a combined circulation of about 24 million. Similar messages were carried in many company publications.

The Institute of Outdoor Advertising also added its efforts to the Advertising Council campaign. Painted bulletins were placed in twenty densely populated metropolitan areas, and nearly 100,000 car cards were sent out for use in buses and other forms of public transportation.

The whole remarkable program was carried out as a public service. The magnitude of the service rendered by the council is indicated by the fact that the promotional materials resulting from the council's efforts alone represented an estimated $10 million in media space and time.

Much additional special work was required to reach the residents of the inner city, even though some parts of the national campaign were aimed at such minorities as the blacks, Puerto Ricans, Spanish Americans, and Chinese. A community education program was developed to inform such people of the importance of filling out the census questionnaires. Much assistance was provided by community agencies and leaders and by the endorsements given by trusted national organizations. Federal agencies with community and neighborhood programs extended assistance through their local representatives in the inner-city areas. Among the special devices employed in this wide-ranging program were sound trucks to cruise the streets, local assistance centers, and exhibits of various kinds.

Publications and Services

The products of the decennial census are so varied and complex that it is almost impossible to adequately inform potential users of the possibilities provided by the full range of information. The printed output alone will be some 200,000 pages, and the amount of tabulated information available on machine-readable tapes is considerably greater than that furnished in published form, since the summary tapes show the population totals for many geographic areas not shown in the published reports. The potentialities for special tabulations to the order of particular users open the door to an even greater amount of tabulated information. It has been estimated that in past censuses the users have never utilized as much as 10 per cent of the material that could have proven helpful.

For a short period after a census, there is a very high degree of awareness of the results. The first local stories regarding the preliminary and final population totals are always widely reported in the local press. The second wave, consisting of more detailed bulletins on the final population counts, is also widely reported to the public, leading to many stories regarding changes in growth rates and comparisons with other areas. The wide attention given the first two waves of material is due to the fact that for any given area only one figure is involved, and its significance is apparent to almost everyone.

The situation is much different for later releases of the census results, which present figures in progressively greater subject detail. Even the simpler subdivisions by age, sex, and color are much less widely reported by the media, partly because of the space or time required, and partly because of the effort needed to interpret the materials. Nevertheless, in the aggregate, there are a good many news stories that analyze the census figures in some depth and call attention to the outstanding changes they reveal. Particular attention is given to stories on the changing distribution of the population by color and other characteristics, on educational gains, on the distribution of income, and on gains in the housing standards.

Broad public awareness of census materials is limited to the conventional printed reports. A much smaller group, including social scientists, researchers, librarians, local planners, and the staffs of information and processing agencies, is acquainted with the output in the form of summary tapes. Many of the smaller groups also know that arrangements can be made to get special tabulations tailored to particular needs.

Those who use data from the census are a very small number in relation to the many millions who answer the questionnaires. Consequently, those with complaints about any kind of reporting burden are much more likely to get political attention than those who wish to have more information. Additional safeguards for the suppliers of data, if indeed such safeguards are needed, can be furnished by giving up some part of the present informational services or by accepting a lower quality of statistical data. The task of finding a wise balance among conflicting alternatives is one requiring both political and statistical statesmanship.

XIII

International Relationships

Statistical work is an important common interest in a world that otherwise has so many bases for conflict and misunderstanding. Statistical data are a necessity, whether the government is democratic or socialist, whether the country is economically advanced or in the early stages of development. In all these situations, the problems faced by a statistician are much the same. At their international meetings, statisticians usually pay little attention to differences in economic organization or social philosophy. Instead, their time is given over completely to such matters as standardization of concepts and definitions, legal and financial support for statistical work, attitudes of respondents, sampling methods, availability of maps, experience with new equipment and software, and a host of other common concerns.

When the International Statistical Institute was organized in 1885, Dr. Francis A. Walker, Superintendent of the 1870 and 1880 censuses was one of the founding members and served as vice-president from 1893 to 1897. Dr. Walter F. Willcox, chief statistician for the 1900 census, was elected to membership in the International Statistical Institute in 1899 and served as vice-president from 1923 to 1947, as president for a short time in 1947, and as honorary president until his death in 1963 at the age of 102.

In 1918, when the American Statistical Association issued a series of essays in honor of its seventy-fifth anniversary, the lead article reviewing worldwide progress in public statistics over the preceding three-quarters of a century was by Dr. Simon N. D. North, Director of the Census from 1903 to 1909, and the article on federal statistics of the United States was by John Cummings of the Census Bureau staff. Similar articles on the statistics of other countries provided an early means for technical exchange among leading countries of the world.

VISITS BY OFFICIALS OF FOREIGN STATISTICAL AGENCIES

Over many years, the technological advances introduced by the Census Bureau have been of great interest to technical personnel in other countries who have visited the Bureau to get firsthand knowledge of its work. A number of the earlier contacts resulted from the development of punched card equipment, which was introduced fairly rapidly in other countries after its first major use in the census of 1890. More recently, visitors have been concerned with the use of electronic computers and associated devices, sampling and survey methods, response research, evaluation of censuses and surveys, and the use of administrative records for statistical purposes.

In 1946, the appointment of Calvert L. Dedrick as Coordinator of International Statistics marked the first time that the Bureau had designated a focal point for all its relationships with foreign statisticians. In view of the many parts of the Bureau interested in international work, it was clear that such a program was needed, not only for visitors from highly organized statistical offices, but also to provide technical assistance to what were then designated as under-developed (or, more recently, as developing) countries. Since the establishment of the program, there have been more than three thousand foreign visitors to the Bureau. Some of the nearly one hundred countries involved have sent the heads of their statistical offices to visit the Bureau in order to gain firsthand information about various plans and programs.

The exchange of official publications has been an important feature of the Bureau's international program. Mailings of appropriate technical documents are made to statistical offices and research organizations in 130 countries. In return for its methodological materials (such as schedules, manuals, procedures, and summary publications), the Bureau receives a steady flow of like materials from abroad. There is no doubt that this kind of exchange has been extremely beneficial in bringing about widespread awareness of advances in the several statistical programs of the Census Bureau.

Contacts with representatives of foreign statistical offices have led to active two-way relationships. Effective cooperation and exchange have taken place with Statistics Canada, formerly the Dominion Bureau of Statistics. In this case, exchange visits by technicians and administrators of both bureaus have been frequent for some twenty years, with opportunities freely offered to observe training programs, pre-tests, technical discussions, and public hearings. As a result, the key statisticians in each country are familiar with a considerable range of developments and problems in the other country. On a number of occasions the result of an experiment in one country has been helpful to the other in giving assurance of workability or in avoiding difficulties. In the case of Australia, because of the distance involved, exchanges have taken a different form. Several key members of the staff of the Commonwealth Bureau of Statistics have spent periods of up to one year at the Census Bureau. The exchange of ideas during such continued periods of contact has been most fruitful, but the range of subjects has often been smaller than in the case of Canada. Somewhat less intensive—but nevertheless helpful—exchanges have taken place with Great Britain, Germany, France, Sweden, Norway, and Israel, and a number of other countries.

It is not easy to estimate the advances attributable to the many consultations and two-way exchanges that have taken place in the past twenty-five years. During this period the Census Bureau has clearly broken new ground in a number of areas, such as the use of electronic equipment, data processing, the extension of sampling to all phases of statistical work, response research, automation of many phases of statistical production, evaluation of censuses and surveys, and preparation of procedural studies. The examples have been followed in a number of other countries, often with modifications that later proved helpful to the Bureau. There is little doubt that technical gains in almost any area are speeded up by the pooling of experience gained in different countries.

THE CENSUS BUREAU IN INTERNATIONAL ORGANIZATIONS

Although Walker and Willcox were early participants in the affairs of the International Statistical Institute, the Census Bureau as well as other statistical agencies of the U.S. Government, had relatively little contact with the institute prior to World War II. In the 1950's and 1960's, representatives of the Bureau participated quite regularly in the sessions of the institute every two years and the Bureau staff was increasingly represented in its membership. For most of these years, the Bureau had an unusually high proportion of the limited number of constituent memberships held by statisticians in the U.S. Government.

In another international organization, the Inter-American Statistical Institute, the Bureau's staff had an important role from its inception. This organization was an outgrowth of an Inter-American Scientific Congress, which met in Washington in 1940. The first Secretary-General was Halbert L. Dunn, Chief of the Division of Vital Statistics, then part of the Bureau. The new organization included as charter members the members of the International Statistical Institute in the United States, Canada, and the Latin American countries. It was intended to provide a regional association for official and other statisticians concerned with promotion of statistical work and standards in all the Western Hemisphere countries. For a number of years the Census Bureau provided space and other assistance for the Inter-American Statistical Institute's secretariat and sponsored an important regional effort in behalf of the Census of the Americas and the World Census of Agriculture of 1950. Technicians of the Census Bureau and colleagues from other Western Hemisphere countries served on a commission to develop minimum standards before the United Nations developed its worldwide program. Efforts put forth at that time brought about considerable improvement in the international comparability of statistics and statistical standards throughout the Americas.

The Census Bureau has also had close and continuing consultation and work relationships with the United Nations and other international agencies, especially the Food and Agriculture Organization and the International Labor Office. The Bureau staff has been involved recurrently in providing technical papers, staff consultation, and in some cases, U.S. representation or technical aid on the U.N. Statistical Commission and the U.N. Population Commission. Bureau representatives have also participated in many international and regional meetings concerned with the development of statistics, and provision of data for international yearbooks and compendia, and in the loan of technicians for special assignments, and the development of joint training programs. Through all these contacts, the Census Bureau has had a significant impact on the guidelines which the U.N. agencies have issued in connection with censuses, surveys, and current statistics.

STATE DEPARTMENT PROGRAMS

The most extensive contacts with foreign countries have been made by the Census Bureau under the programs of the Agency for International Development and its predecessor organizations. These programs have taken two forms: (1) advisory services by Bureau personnel stationed abroad to work with foreign government agencies and (2) training of foreign statistical personnel in the United States.

The total number of persons trained at the Census Bureau since 1946 is nearly two thousand, drawn from 80 countries. It is noteworthy that there have been 500 trainees from countries in Southern Asia, such as Thailand, India, Pakistan, and Indonesia, and nearly half as many from the Philippines, Korea, and Nationalist China. Until 1951, when the Point Four Program was inaugurated, the training programs were carried out under a scientific and cultural cooperation program, which was limited to Latin American countries. Since then, the Bureau's training activities have been extended to developing countries in both hemispheres. During the 1950's, many of the new participants in the program came from the Near East and the Far East, and in the 1960's an increasing amount of training was given to nationals from a number of African countries.

The training programs have varied widely with respect to subjects covered, length of assignments, and arrangements for instruction. The needs of each foreign statistician or other specialist are carefully evaluated, and an effort is made to develop a program in the light of individual needs. Thus, if the group being trained consists of heads of statistical offices or other key officials, considerable emphasis is placed on planning, public policy, and broad administration. On the other hand, those who will be in charge of a specific function, such as sampling, mapping, or tabulation, are given some experience with the technical operations involved in such work. Individual training programs vary roughly from a month to two years or more and include academic studies. Classes consist of one or two persons when a highly specialized program is involved but may include as many as 30. The subjects cover a variety of fields—sampling, mapping, field organization and management, data processing, broad census and survey planning, and foreign trade statistics. The arrangements for instruction have involved not only classes and individual projects at the Bureau of the Census but also attendance at appropriate universities and specialized training in other statistical agencies, such as the Bureau of Labor Statistics, the Bureau of Economic Analysis and the National Center for Health Statistics.

In the past several years, the training program has been modified in a number of ways. Cooperative arrangements with international agencies, such as the Food and Agriculture Organization, have made possible the assembly of a stronger combination of technical and material resources devoted to training. A case-study approach has been developed to provide materials relating to the conduct of a census or sample survey in a mythical country having a set of characteristics similar to those of the home countries of participants. These simulated case-study materials are presented in "workshops" at the Bureau and abroad, and have been translated into Spanish, Turkish, Farsi, Chinese, and other foreign languages. This has made the program accessible to a larger number of participants and, in some cases, has provided opportunities for field testing that would be difficult to duplicate in the United States.

The second broad class of Bureau assistance to foreign countries—the extending of consulting services—dates back to 1939 but was not employed extensively until the late 1940's. In the past twenty-five years, a total of sixty-five countries have received some statistical advisory service from members of the Bureau staff. Before an adviser undertakes an extended assignment in the country, it has been found advantageous to have some of the staff members of a foreign statistical office trained in the Census Bureau. The resulting cadre of workers, familiar with some of the Bureau's procedures, facilitates the work of the adviser and provides some assurance of continuity after his departure.

Census Bureau advisers have provided some form of technical assistance to more than twenty countries undertaking their first censuses of population. They have also been consulted on the planning and execution of housing censuses, agricultural censuses, and economic censuses, and have participated actively in the installation of large-scale sample household surveys.

A consultant's work may be very broad in nature or may relate to quite specific statistical tasks, such as mapping, field organization, or tabulation. The length of the assignment for a particular individual may be as short as a few weeks when a technical follow-up or a reconnaissance of a particular problem is being undertaken. On the other hand, two to six years are generally needed for a sizable census program to be organized and carried out. In many cases, the consultant is called on for advice regarding the problems of creating or modernizing a central statistical organization. He may help in the legislative and budgetary planning for such an office and may serve for a time as special adviser to the director of statistics. The objective in all cases is not to have the consultant do the work for the local people but rather to create in the host country an experienced staff and organization to do the necessary statistical work.

Services rendered by consultants have varied with technical developments in the advanced countries. In the earlier years, tabulation advice was largely directed toward the use of conventional punched card equipment. More recently, the officials in developing countries have been eager to acquire electronic equipment for data processing. Consultants frequently advise them on the installation of types of equipment consistent with the needs of the country and the supply of technical manpower and resources available.

RESULTS OF INTERNATIONAL PROGRAMS

Since 1946, the total expenditures under the various Bureau programs for extending technical assistance to foreign countries have amounted to some $15 million. A quantitative appraisal of the results is difficult. In some cases, the officials who have been trained do not continue in the government service but leave their posts for university or other work. Even so, the benefits to the country may be considerable, since the lack of trained personnel in the universities and in business often holds back national development. In the case of the consultants, evaluation of the results is likewise difficult. A consultant is most effective when he operates in a supporting capacity to the local officials with whom he is working. His role is a facilitating one—helping others deal with obstacles in achieving their objectives.

One approach used to indicate the value of the training program was to take an individual group of trainees and follow their progress over subsequent years. This was done more than ten years ago by the National Planning Association in an effort to determine the contribution being made by technical cooperation programs. The study was based upon twenty-eight statisticians from fifteen countries of Latin America, who came to the United States in 1947 under a training program for the 1950 Census of the Americas. Nearly all of the trainees returned to their posts and remained active in statistics until their national censuses had been completed in 1953 and 1954. Nineteen were still in statistical work eight years after the completion of their training program; three of them were then serving with international agencies; five were directors general, or assistant directors general, of statistics in their home countries; six were in charge of a major statistical office; and five were serving in other capacities in statistical work. The most conspicuous member of this group is doubtless Tulo Montenegro from Brazil, who, since 1955, has been the Secretary General of the Inter-American Statistical Institute and has profoundly influenced statistical work in Central and South America.

In the consultation area, it is difficult to avoid the *post hoc, ergo propter hoc* fallacy. Nevertheless, we may examine the developments in several countries where consultants have worked long enough to permit the presumption that the impact of the consultants may be identified. In Turkey there were over thirty different consulting assignments involving a total of forty man-years. During this period, the statistical system was substantially overhauled, and a new statistical law was enacted providing the basis for the establishment of a state institute of statistics with statutory authority for the conduct of centralized statistical functions in Turkey. The increased national recognition of statistics was reflected in higher budgets for such work, in the provision of a special structure for statistical work, and in the development of a national statistical training system.

In Iran there were twenty-two consulting assignments, representing more than thirty man-years. The leader of the advisory group and his American consultants had important responsibilities in connection with the planning, enumeration, processing, and publication phases of the first full population census of Iran in 1956, and, nine years later, the same leader returned for the second census in 1966. He was helpful in enabling local officials to overcome the obstacles that always handicap any new statistical project, and the fact that he spoke

French and acquired a working knowledge of the native language (Farsi) contributed greatly to the quality of the publications for these censuses.

In Thailand, with a total of thirty man-years of consulting service, the Central Statistical Office has been elevated and redesignated the National Statistical Office. The office reports directly to the Prime Minister and has responsibility for co-ordinating all statistical work in the country. In recognition and appreciation of his work, the first chief consultant was given a Citation of the Order of the White Elephant, the highest award that can be granted a foreigner.

Evidence of a successful consultation program can be seen in the creation of a statistical system by Sierra Leone, which has received about fifteen man-years of service since the early 1960's. At the time of independence, this new African country had no statistical law and no local personnel with experience in statistical work. With the help of a senior consultant from the Bureau, there was established a Central Statistical Office, and the first major operation was a population census. This required the installation of data processing equipment, which soon became a central facility for other government agencies, including accounting and billing for the electric utility. Statistics were soon set up in other fields, such as education, labor, agriculture, foreign trade, and railways.

In most developing countries that have participated in the training and consultation program, quantitative evidence regarding benefits may be difficult to find. Nevertheless, for most of these countries, results have more than justified the relatively modest investment in training and consultation.

XIV

Controversies and Conflicts

Thanks to the checks and balances built into our system of government, the conflicts that occur within the governmental organization are usually brought out into the open. These may develop simply as a result of supervisory relationships or because of the normal exercise of review responsibility. Most of these differences are usually resolved quite rapidly. In some cases, however, the Bureau of the Census has been involved in a controversy for a year or more, and the impact has been significant.

Two examples of such continuing conflict have already been described (in Chapters II and X). The protracted struggle between the Secretary of the Department and the Director of the Bureau in the early 1900's may bear some analogy to the fable of the dog and his shadow. The Director apparently became so preoccupied with retaining the prerogatives enjoyed in a previous Department that he damaged his effectiveness in presenting the case for strengthening the role of the Census Bureau. Another conflict took place when Eisenhower's Secretary proved to be quite willing to let Congress withhold funds for the periodic censuses of business and manufactures. The Secretary's views regarding these censuses would surely have prevailed except for the rapid marshaling of counterforces by business and other organizations.

A third conflict, this one between branches of the federal government, took place during the Eightieth Congress, which convened in February, 1947. In 1947 and 1948, the appropriation requests of the agencies were frequently subjected to "Taberization," a term based on the name of the chairman of the House Appropriations Committee, Congressman John Taber. All parts of the Census request were scrutinized in detail and, for two successive years, the base for the program of current statistics was sharply reduced, as the committee pressed for the elimination of many current statistical series and for a reduction in frequency and detail of the remainder. The vigor of their attack is shown by the fact that funds for the fiscal year 1948 were about 40 per cent below those for 1947, and in the next year there was a further decrease of nearly 10 per cent. Funds were completely cut off for the 1946 Census of Religious Bodies, even though much of the collection work had already been completed. As a result of the extremely sharp curtailment, the Bureau was compelled to carry out a reduction of force that eliminated many of the younger professional and technical staff. It was possible to repair most of the program damage within a few years, but the adverse effects of severe personnel cuts were reflected in the shortage of "middle management" people for the next decade or two.

The plans of the Census Bureau and the statistics it publishes are often under attack by a particular class of the population or by the people in a particular geographic area. It is a tribute to both the public and the Bureau that these differences ordinarily do not involve any considerable numbers of people. There have been two notable exceptions, however, when the initial concern spread rapidly, and congressional hearings were called for. Both cases arose in connection with the population census, and both were the result of a campaign initiated by a member of Congress who had not been widely known previously.

THE INCOME CONTROVERSY

Sometime prior to the taking of the 1940 census, it became obvious that information on income was badly needed. After a period of prolonged unemployment, it was clear that simple counts of persons out of work would not be a sufficient measure of the problem. Many people were working at unsuitable jobs or at substandard wages. Data on income, as well as on age, occupation, industry, and hours of work, were needed for measuring the unemployment problem. It was appreciated also that the business uses of income data would be considerable, since such data would provide businessmen with a picture of their markets and a basis for their distribution plans.

When the printing of the 1940 schedules began in 1939, there was no basis for forecasting the eruption that was to take place early in the next year. Indeed, the sensitivity of the public on this question had been seriously underestimated. The strong resistance which showed up in later years in Canada, Great Britain, and Australia, where census traditions and economic development generally parallel our own, suggests that the innovation here entailed real hazards.

There were two fortunate aspects of the census program, but they did not become obvious until later. First, the inquiry was a very modest one calling for little except wage and salary income. For persons receiving $5,000 and over, it was sufficient to report that income was $5,000 or more. Those with income from other sources were asked merely to report whether it was in excess of $50 per year. The second fortuitous feature was the limited period for public discussion. The first news reports of the census plans to ask about income appeared only about a year before the date of the census. The next publicity occurred in the summer of 1939 when the questions were being tested in St. Joseph and Marshall counties, Indiana. During the remainder of the year, there was little evidence of widespread public concern about the income questions.

It remained for Senator Charles W. Tobey of New Hampshire to exploit the issue early in 1940. On January 3, 1940, Tobey appeared on the Senate floor to read a letter to the Secretary of Commerce, denouncing the plans of the census to collect information on income and requesting the Secretary to eliminate questions on this subject. The Secretary refused to comply, and on February 7, Tobey introduced Senate Resolution 231, identified as a "Resolution favoring the deletion from the Sixteenth Census Population Schedule of inquiries numbered 32 and 33 relating to compensation received." On February 19, the senator presented his case to a nationwide audience in a radio address, in which the theme of census snooping was dominant. Alleged scandals while Hopkins was administrator of the Work Projects Administration were cited to show the hazards of giving information to enumerators recruited through political channels. Tobey called the questions unconstitutional and in violation of the Bill of Rights, which was intended to protect against unreasonable searches and seizures. His final point was that the census questions lacked legislative authority, since the 1929 Census Act restricted the inquiries to specific topics, such as population, unemployment, and certain other subjects. Tobey asked for public assistance in his campaign, and referred to support for his cause in resolutions adopted at a mass meeting of the housewives of Olean, New York. He closed with the exhortation: "Eternal vigilance is still the price of liberty. Stand up and fight."

This appeal apparently had considerable effect, for less than ten days after, in the Senate hearing on his resolution, Tobey reported the receipt of some 4,000 letters. In a number of cases, these represented the views of groups such as the Defenders of America (from Pittsburgh) and the Fairfield (New Hampshire) Grange. Others were signed by groups of citizens from a particular community. The greatest response was from New England, but replies came from as far away as San Diego, California. There were a number of newspaper stories in behalf of the Tobey resolution. Articles by Arthur Krock, a columnist for the *New York Times,* led to a series of published communications between the Director of the Census and Krock. The effect of Krock's statements was offset, in part at least, by a column in favor of the income questions under the by-line of a rival columnist, Dorothy Thompson.

The hearings on Tobey's resolution extended over a period of three days around the end of February. Supporters of the resolution included seven other members of Congress and spokesmen for the Sentinels of the Republic, Women Investors in America, Inc., and the National Association of American War Mothers. One woman came from Kenmore, New York, to report on a county-wide meeting of seven-hundred women, all ready to go to jail rather than answer the income questions.

The witnesses against the resolution included Bureau and Department representatives who testified in detail about the need for the income questions and the extent of public support. Successful experience in collecting income data was reported, with particular emphasis upon the results of the pre-test about six months earlier in Indiana. The legality of the inquiries was justified on the basis that income is definitely a subject relating to unemployment, a view supported by the fact that the Congress three years earlier, in setting up the 1937 National Unemployment Census, included a question on total individual income, cash and other. In response to the concern about giving personal information to census takers, the government representatives stressed the record of the Census Bureau in maintaining confidentiality. The census inquiries were also supported by representatives of the National Consumers' League, the Congress of Industrial Organizations, and a consultant on distribution who had served on a Bureau advisory committee.

Fortunately, the Census Bureau developed a proposal shortly after the hearings that proved to be a very good compromise. Both in Tobey's major radio speech and in the letters that followed, the major issue raised was the possibility that information given to the enumerators would not be protected. The Census proposed, therefore, that all households should be given an opportunity to report income on a separate form to be mailed directly to Washington. The availability of a separate report form was probably the reason why the Senate leadership did not bring up the Tobey resolution for action by the Senate, even though the committee had reported favorably upon it.

The outcome was most gratifying, as far as the Bureau was concerned. Out of a total of 15 million forms printed, less than 200,000 were used, some not because of the requests from respondents but because enumerators found it convenient to leave the form to avoid call-backs on respondents unable to supply the income information at the time of the enumerator's visit.

THE 1970 CENSUS

Hyman Alterman, in a recent book (*Counting People: The Census in History*), has referred to the 1970 census as the census of controversy. In this case, unlike the situation three decades earlier, there was ample time to consider amending the legislation providing legislative authority for the census. The dispute concerned not one or two questions, but the broad scope and authority for the census as a whole.

Inasmuch as the controversy actually began early in 1967, it would be easy to regard it as an outgrowth of hearings and public discussion regarding wiretapping, electronic eavesdropping, and similar invasions of privacy. In 1966, the first discussion of proposals for a National Data Bank had suggested the possibility that information collected in some future census might be put into such a central file.

A somewhat different explanation is offered in a story by Nan Robertson in the *New York Times* for April 1, 1969. She reported that in the campaign year 1966, Congressman Jackson Betts was visiting his home district in Ohio, when he received a complaint from a retired couple who had become alarmed about the efforts of a census enumerator to collect data. He concluded that the census could make a good campaign issue because it touches the lives of so many citizens and asked his assistant to look into the matter.

If we accept this story, the result was reflected in a bill, H.R. 10952, introduced by Betts on June 20, 1967, which limited the mandatory authority of the Census Bureau to ask questions on name and address, relationship, sex, race, marital status, and visitors in household at the time of the census. The response to all other questions would be made voluntary.

A day later, Betts appeared before the Subcommittee on Census and Statistics of the House Post Office and Civil Service Committee. His deceptively mild statement at the outset, "I am not conducting a crusade" gave no hint of the fact that for the next three years his name would be associated with little else but decennial census legislation. The arguments in behalf of his bill were to be repeated many times in the next two or three years. In brief, Congress had failed to keep the census within proper bounds, citizens had been deprived of their right to privacy by being compelled to answer too many questions, and the undercount in 1960 had been due to the burdensome schedule and the penalties.

Betts also referred to the proposed National Data Bank and charged that it would provide "complete files on everything about a person."

In September 1967, Betts informed the Congress of the results of inquiries he had directed to a list of marketing firms and to the attorneys general of the states. The companies indicated their ability to collect valid information on a voluntary basis, and nearly all of the states reported that their population and housing information is collected without the use of mandatory authority. What Betts did not bring out, to be sure, was that private firms, which must base all of their work upon voluntary responses, could not be expected to indicate any lack of ability to collect the data they need. The report also failed to point out the fact that the true rate of response in private surveys might reach at best 80 per cent and that this level was attainable only in a survey based on personal interviews. In many private surveys, the rate of response is very much below 80 percent. In the case of the inquiry addressed to the states, the absence of mandatory authority has little significance, since practically none of them collect either population or housing information by direct canvass. Most of their estimates are based upon data from administrative records, such as births and deaths, school attendance, and building permits. There is only one state, Massachusetts, which takes an enumerative census, and for this there is mandatory authority. In Kansas, some population data are collected in connection with assessment.

The next step in the Betts campaign was the presentation of comprehensive recommendations on the content of the 1970 census, appearing in the *Congressional Record* for October 4, 1967. In this proposal, which went far beyond the Betts Bill, about two-thirds of the major questions in the 1970 census program would have been eliminated as being of primarily local or commercial interest or simply not important enough for inclusion in a national census. Except for the seven required questions, all the inquiries would have applied only to a sample of perhaps 3 million households.

On October 24, 1967, hearings on H.R. 10952 took place before the Subcommittee on Census and Statistics of the House Post Office and Civil Service Committee. Betts at that time referred to the proposed use of the mails for the 1970 census as an additional point in support of his proposal. He argued that application of mandatory authority to the entire schedule was likely to cause some citizens to fail to return their forms. A shorter and simpler form, in his opinion, would lead to better responses from the public. Congressman Cornelius Gallagher, chairman of the Special Subcommittee on Invasion of Privacy, the only other witness to testify before the committee, disagreed with Betts on the reduction of mandatory authority, stating, "Mr. Chairman, this is one instance in which I believe that the government's need to know overcomes the possible intrusions into a citizen's right to privacy." He did, however, agree that Congress should exercise closer supervision over the inquiries made by the Census Bureau.

Fortunately for the Census Bureau, Congressman William Green, the chairman of the Subcommittee on Census and Statistics, was apparently not disposed to push the legislation introduced by Betts. His earlier agreement to have a hearing was a matter of public record. Gallagher, whose record showed that he was for the protection of privacy but not in favor of reducing mandatory authority, was given a chance to appear immediately after Betts. Exhibits offered for the record by Betts were not accepted routinely, as is often done as a matter of courtesy to another member, but only on a selective basis, lest the record become too voluminous. The subcommittee never prepared a report on the Betts legislation, even though there was some internal pressure for such action. In addition, the printing of the hearing, late in 1968, included some fifty pages devoted to communications from planning agencies, health departments, and state and local officials concerned with possible reduction in the usefulness of the 1970 census.

By the end of 1967, Betts had laid a solid base for his campaign. About fifteen bills identical or similar to his had been introduced in the House. Nevertheless, there may have been some disappointment over the rate of progress, for in December, 1967, his office issued to his congressional colleagues a "Dear Friend" letter suggesting that the probing personal inquiries of the 1970 census provided a good "people" issue and thus would be a good subject for releases and newsletters in January, which otherwise might be a slow month.

The year 1968 was to bring about a considerable increase in the number of congressmen supporting Betts by sponsoring similar legislation. By the end of the year, the number had risen to forty-six, about four-fifths of them from the Republican side. Among the bills introduced were three that would have put the entire census of agriculture on a voluntary basis. A somewhat different type of bill was offered by Senator John G. Tower, who apparently hoped to end the controversy by requiring the Secretary of Commerce to limit inquiries to categories essential to accomplish the purposes of the census.

Two developments during 1968 may have contributed to the rise in the number of Betts' supporters. In February, the results of a poll of the National Federation of Independent Business became available showing that 83 per cent of those responding favored Betts' legislation and 13 per cent opposed it. Later, in time set aside at Betts' request for House discussion of the Census issue, twenty congressmen appeared on the floor to present statements in favor of the legislation, and another twenty-five submitted supporting statements for the record.

Field tests of census procedures in 1968 provided an appraisal not only of new procedures, but also of the ability of the field organization to cope with the negative influence of advice to citizens that they should resist the census. The test in Dane County, Wisconsin (including the city of Madison), was accompanied by a newspaper advertisement and a letter to citizens, both financed by a National Right to Privacy Committee, and both urging them to speak out against the harassment represented by the census test. Nevertheless, possibly as a result of all the publicity, the rate of mail response reached a record high of 90 per cent. In a test in Chesterfield and Sumter counties of South Carolina, Senator Strom Thurmond, a supporter of the Betts legislation —and apparently unaware of the legal sanctions for a census pre-test—erroneously advised citizens of their right to decline to furnish answers. Despite the advice from the senator, which was followed by some local publicity opposing the inquiries, the test in the two counties was carried out successfully, with no significant adverse reaction from respondents.

One important development in the fall of 1968 was the position taken by the American Civil Liberties Union regarding the Betts legislation. This organization, which has a long history of concern with the rights of citizens and means of protecting them against invasion of privacy, concluded that all questions on the decennial census should be compulsory except for race. The exception was made because some people "feel threatened by discrimination by having to answer race questions" and because of the belief that the question had an inadequate formulation and should be improved and systematized. It would be difficult to explain, on other than political considerations, why so many conservative congressmen should be more concerned than the American Civil Liberties Union about the privacy of individual citizens.*

* Claus Moser, the Chief Statistician in Great Britain, recently commented that many of the complaints about privacy in his country come from people who wish the government to have less power.

An important result of the increased congressional support for Betts in 1968 was that some of the users of census data began to take seriously the threat implied by the proposed legislation. In 1967, and during much of 1968, it was thought that passage of the legislation was so unlikely that efforts to refute the charges did not seem to be necessary. Fortunately, one small but influential group, the Federal Statistics Users' Conference, the only private organization to concentrate its attention on federal statistics, was alert to the danger from the outset. Its representative, usually Executive Director John Aiken, testified at a number of congressional hearings on the views of the members, and its newsletters alerted other organizations concerned about the availability of census data. Some newspaper stories and magazine articles in opposition to the legislation began to appear in 1968, but the bulk of the published materials continued to feature the standard attacks against the census questions, the unreasonable nature of the penalties for not answering, and the possibilities for misuse of the data collected.

On the other hand, evidence of the beginning of a favorable tide was provided by many of the letters to the Post Office and Civil Service Committee. By the time the record of the 1967 hearings was published, it included about one hundred letters in opposition to the Betts Bill from such sources as the American Public Health Association, Governor Nelson A. Rockefeller of New York, regional and local planning groups, chambers of commerce, public health agencies, universities, research groups, and many kinds of businesses.

Early in 1969, the year of climax in the three-year controversy, several events occurred that must have been encouraging to the proponents of restrictive census legislation. First of all, Betts modified his bill in two ways. Apparently with a bow to the Senate for passing a bill in 1968 eliminating all jail penalties, he introduced this feature in his bill.

He also removed the subject of race from the mandatory list, possibly because this was the one question which the American Civil Liberties Union would not make mandatory. The number associated in sponsorship of the new legislation rose to one hundred by the end of January, and later reached 145, one-third of the entire membership of the House.

Betts' immediate office continued to be the focal point for the drive to secure enough support to pass the legislation. The case was supported mainly by repetition of the kind of charges already made. Reference was continually made to a total of 117 questions, despite the fact that this total could be obtained only by adding all the different inquiries on the forms designed for 80 per cent of the population, those for 15 per cent, and those for 5 per cent. A number of the questions appeared on one form only, and the maximum number of questions for any individual was actually less than ninety. The question on whether the bathroom was shared continued to be distorted into the much more interesting version "With whom do you share your shower?" A new note was the emphasis now placed on the "unwholesome alliance" between the Census Bureau and federal users, probably to be taken as a tribute to the growing effectiveness of the Federal Statistics Users' Conference in bringing public attention to the controversy.

Even though the support for Betts may have been somewhat eroded by articles in *Advertising Age, Nation's Business,* and in some of the publications of the University Bureaus of Business and Economic Research, as well as by other articles by supporters of the Census Bureau, it is probable that their effect was more than offset by the output of a number of pro-Betts columnists and commentators, including Dan Smoot, Reverend Carl MacIntire, Martin Gross, Paul Harvey, and Dean Manion, as well as a statement on behalf of the Liberty Lobby.

It is quite possible that the optimism that Betts voiced late in 1968 regarding the prospects for his bill in 1969 was based in part on the hope that changes made by the new Nixon Administration would be helpful. Indeed, one newspaper story suggested that perhaps the new President could end the census row by appointing a Director more favorable to Betts' viewpoint. Any possible hopes he may have had for Administration cooperation were short-lived, however, for the new Secretary of Commerce, Maurice Stans, made it clear in a February hearing before the Joint Economic Committee that he would strongly oppose the Betts legislation. The Secretary soon took an active role in the controversy, and in a letter to all members of Congress on April 18, 1969, announced some changes both for the short and the long run. The immediate changes included a reduction in the number of households to get the longer form, and a rewording of the overworked bathroom question to avoid any implication of simultaneous double use. In the longer run, the Secretary agreed to have questions for future censuses submitted to the Congress two years in advance and to appoint a blue ribbon committee to look into such matters as sampling and the use of voluntary response. (This committee, known as the Decennial Census Review Committee to the Secretary of Commerce, appointed late in 1969, submitted a report in the summer of 1971 that strongly affirmed the importance of the decennial census and the need for mandatory authority for carrying it out.)

Hearings on the legislation began on April 1, 1969, before the newly reconstituted Subcommittee on Census and Statistics of the House Post Office and Civil Service Committee. The group was described in a *New York Times* headline as "Hostile Census Unit." The hearing before this subcommittee was the most intensive and gruelling that this writer, in his capacity as Director of the Census, ever faced, since it covered reasons for many of the questions, final responsibility for selection of questions, and the possibility of bias against educational questions in favor of housing statistics. Inquiries about what action would be taken if the proposed legislation were enacted and a warning against spending any money unnecessarily while the bill was under discussion were especially difficult. The attitude of the subcommittee was not surprising, for four of its eight members were co-sponsors of the legislation. The Director, who was at that time awaiting the designation of his successor, would have found it even more difficult to respond to some of the inquiries, except for the demonstrated strong support of the new Secretary. In addition, all of the departments to which the bill had been referred had objected to it in very strong terms.

In five days of hearings in Washington, Betts and other congressmen for and against the bill were given a chance to testify or to submit a written statement. Representatives of the Office of Management and Budget and four departments testified to the damage that would result from enactment of the legislation. Hearings were also held in Los Angeles and San Francisco, California and in Vienna, Virginia to obtain the views of local citizens regarding the 1970 census plans.

By the time the hearings had been completed, the chairman and some of his associates had been exposed to a number of influences that precluded reporting out the original bill. The amount of local support for the legislation was less than expected, bearing out Chairman Charles H. Wilson's view, as expressed at the opening of the hearings on April 1, that much of the outcry appeared to have been "deliberately fomented." One witness who had been scheduled to appear in support of the legislation admitted that he had learned from earlier witnesses that his prepared statement was incorrect. The strong and unanimous opposition of the departments brought further doubts as to the wisdom of doing anything to jeopardize the forthcoming census. The concessions made by the Secretary helped reduce the pressures, and finally the Census

Bureau's testimony concerning the inevitable reduction of quality and escalation of costs affected the views of subcommittee members.

Although the subcommittee was not prepared to eliminate mandatory authority for the census, there was a consensus in favor of the changes embodied in a new bill, H.R. 12884, drafted to take account of a number of issues brought out in the hearings. The most significant features of the new bill were the retention of the mandatory authority with the fine retained (but not the jail sentence), the introduction of specific requirements for congressional review and approval of questions, and the tightening up of the confidentiality provisions. The bill was approved by the committee in July and by the House in September, 1969. It is noteworthy that even at that late date, about six months before the census was to start, Betts failed by only a narrow margin (123 to 107) in getting House approval of an amendment which would have removed the mandatory authority from all but six questions. The narrow margin indicates that except for the alert membership of the Federal Statistics Users' Conference, as well as other informed users of census data, the House would have enacted legislation that would have had most unfortunate results. The legislation was not taken up by the Senate and hence the bill died with the expiration of the Ninety-first Congress.

The 1970 census once again demonstrated how little public cooperation is actually affected by controversy, even when the controversy is extensive. Eighty-seven per cent of the households in the mail areas sent in their forms before it was necessary to have an enumerator call, a figure 5 per cent above the level budgeted in advance. The quality of the response was likewise fully up to expectations. There was little resistance to requests for cooperation, and there is reason to believe that the coverage was a little better than in 1960, despite economic and social factors that could have caused a much greater relative undercount.

It is probably too much to hope that the controversy over mandatory authority came to an end with the 1970 census. Indeed, the success of the 1970 census, the high degree of cooperation extended to enumerators, and the infrequency with which legal sanctions proved necessary will be cited as proof that citizens will meet their responsibilities regardless of any legal compulsion to do so.

XV

The Future of the Bureau

The simplest, and sometimes the best, way to predict the future of an organization is to make an extrapolation of its past record. This approach is especially appropriate for an agency administering a program applying to a limited (statistical) universe, with fairly consistent year-to-year changes. The Bureau of the Census, however, does not fit this category. In its long history, it has evolved from a temporary organization with only one kind of census to a permanent organization conducting various kinds of censuses and surveys throughout each decade. In the last thirty years, numerous programs have been added to supply current statistics between periodic censuses, and more recently, a large amount of service work has been undertaken for other agencies. In this situation, extrapolation is difficult, and it is better to give broad attention to the probable nature of the demand and supply functions for statistical work in our economy.

ASSUMPTIONS

In any look ahead, it has become accepted practice to outline the assumptions that form the basis for the predictions.

This enables the reader to modify projected developments on the basis of his own assumptions.

The first, and perhaps the central assumption, is that the demand for statistical information will continue to increase rapidly. This is an inevitable concomitant of the growing size and complexity of a nation in which the interdependence of individuals and institutions is constantly increasing. Government and business decisions will be based to an even greater extent upon the results of statistical inquiries carefully designed to apply to specific requirements. Regardless of whether the applications are made inside or outside of the government, regardless of the extent of use of operations research agencies, and regardless of the techniques used (model building, index numbers, time series analysis, multivariate analysis), most of the building blocks required will be statistical facts derived from censuses and surveys, often supplemented by data from administrative records.

The growing use of statistics will bring a disproportionate rise in the responsibility of producing agencies. There will be a demand not only for data, but also for all the information needed to use them intelligently. This includes full information on sampling and nonsampling errors, other limitations, and specific factors affecting the interpretation of a particular figure, including its relation to other similar information. When movements can be explained in terms of purely statistical factors or of some unusual event, the producer will be expected to make this information available to the user.

It can be taken for granted that the producers of statistics will feel great pressure to increase the efficiency of their work, since funds available for statistics will not rise at a rate commensurate with the growth in demand. This should provide a climate favorable to research efforts in methods and equipment, areas that have proved so productive for many years. It is assumed also that the way will be open to further increases in the amount of service work, provided funds continue to be saved as a result of centralization of collection and tabulation functions.

It is further assumed that the fullest use will be made of administrative records to ensure maximum reduction of the burden on the public. Comparisons between records and data from censuses and surveys not only shed light upon characteristics of the population served by various public programs but also reveal the limitations of certain kinds of census and survey data. Even if the above assumption regarding the use of records is challenged by further controversy over invasion of privacy, the importance of the objectives should make it possible to introduce whatever safeguards are necessary to gain public acceptance.

One final assumption is that the Bureau of the Census will be sufficiently free from sectoral goals to assure that its role in meeting broad national objectives will not be hampered. This assumption would be more easily realized with some form of reorganization but does not depend upon it. For example, as long as the Bureau of the Census continues as a part of the Department of Commerce—or of some other department, such as the proposed Department of Economic Affairs—the Office of Management and Budget could share with the Department the task of shaping the policy of the Census Bureau to recognize fully the over-all needs of government.

INCREASED EMPHASIS ON CURRENT STATISTICS

In the last three decades, the importance of the periodic censuses has been declining significantly in relation to the program of annual, quarterly, and monthly series of intercensal statistics. This trend will persist. Perhaps the major reason is the strong demand for current facts as a basis for current decisions. Over twenty years ago the case was made succinctly by Frederick Mills and Clarence Long in the following words: "In appraising the work of the statistical agencies of Government, account must be taken of the needs of a modern society for accurate current information concerning the processes of economic and social life."

With the development of efficient sampling techniques, many series of current statistics for the nation and broad regions have been developed, but comparatively little has been done so far to provide such information for smaller areas. There is reason to believe that the supply of current statistics for such areas will be increased, thanks to administrative records and the extension of data collection by mail. These features, plus continued improvements in sampling techniques, should make possible much more information on at least an annual basis for counties and the larger cities. The use of administrative records should not be limited to those within the federal system but should include state and local sources. The possibilities for the latter will be materially increased by the establishment of central record systems in some of the states. The growing acceptance of the need for standard classification systems and the adoption of comparable standards and procedures will, of course, broaden the usefulness of local records.

At least a part of the general shift from use of censuses to application of current measures reflects the fact that censuses have become an increasingly inefficient means of meeting current needs for information. As far as population and housing data are concerned, the census train pulls out of the station only once a decade, and there is a great temptation for everyone to pile on board, especially when an alternate means of transportation is not available. The result is that the total number of different questions tends to increase steadily, and the burden on the average respondent can be held down only by means of a complicated sampling design. Because of their size and the need for wide publicity, the periodic censuses are quite vulnerable to attack, as revealed by the controversies of 1940 and 1970. A further disability of the censuses is that all the operations are time-consuming, with the result that the information is often not current by the time it is published. This limitation is particularly serious for small local areas, some of which, because of new construction or other developments, may change very substantially within a few months. A final disability of the traditional census is that the extreme peaks in work loads and numbers of temporary employees make it an inherently inefficient operation.

This has been particularly the case with the collection phase of the decennial census, even with the substantial use of the mails in 1970. The burden of recruiting, testing, and training more than 150,000 temporary field workers is tremendous. Their time of service is so short that most of the work is done by people who are still gaining in speed and efficiency by the time their work is completed. To a less extreme degree, this is also true of the professional and clerical staff who work on the processing of the returns and prepare the results for public use. Most of the workers in statistical operations come to the end of their assignment when they are beginning to be fully proficient in their duties, and the Bureau then loses its investment in training.

Fortunately, the shift in emphasis from censuses to current statistics has a two-way effect in improving the efficiency of operations. It provides some spreading of the work over the decade and thus fills in some of the extreme depressions in Bureau employment. An accompanying reduction in the size of the census at the same time would reduce the height of the decennial peak. Thus, the task of training a somewhat smaller number of workers at peak periods may be carried out with a cadre of supervisory personnel drawn from a larger number of permanent workers in the Bureau.

THE DEMOGRAPHIC PROGRAM

At the present time, there is much too wide a spread between the decennial census, providing details based upon the coverage of all households, and Current Population Survey, which provides monthly figures collected from fifty thousand households. The latter gives information only for the nation as a whole and for extremely broad regions. No figures are given for individual locations. This comparatively inefficient distribution of statistical resources will be modified in future years.

A part of the plan might well be a reduction of the census to the most basic population and housing items. The total number of questions in the census might be limited to a range of fifteen to twenty-five. With the decennial enumeration thus reduced, it would be easier to get authorization and funds for a mid-decade census. The next important step would be the initiation of a series of annual sample surveys or sample censuses to measure intercensal changes and to fill the gap left by the reduction in the scope of the censuses. These would cover a wide range of social and economic items pertaining to the population, as well as detailed information on the characteristics of dwelling units. The samples for these annual surveys should be large enough to yield a considerable amount of information for states, as well as for cities and Standard Metropolitan Statistical Areas with at least 100,000 inhabitants. Through rotation of the inquiries from year to year, information could be obtained on many subjects not feasible to include in the decennial censuses. With the much smaller scale of operations, results could be published much more rapidly. Availability of annual bench marks would reveal changes in the economy much more rapidly and thus provide a better basis for business and government policies. The samples for the annual surveys might be of uniform size each year or might be enlarged in alternate years to give greater geographical or subject detail.

THE ECONOMIC PROGRAM

Future developments in this area must take into account the fact that a considerable number of censuses and surveys are already provided. The censuses generally are on a five-year basis; there are a number of annual surveys, including the well-known annual survey of manufactures, and there are many monthly and quarterly series.

The possibilities for improvements in the economic area are nevertheless considerable, chiefly because of the opportunity for greater exploitation of the administrative records of the Social Security Administration and Internal Revenue Service. This would open the way for a program of annual economic statistics going well beyond the fields covered by the economic censuses, and the creation of an industrial directory applicable to the needs not only of the Census Bureau but also of other statistical agencies of the government. These gains could be paid for in the main by the diversion of some of the funds now going into the five-year censuses, with the result that the amount of information per dollar expended would be substantially increased.

The base for these developments in the coming years is the information on some 8 million enterprises included in the files of the Social Security Administration and Internal Revenue Service. Some 7.9 million of these apply to single-establishment companies doing one kind of business at one location. For all these companies, information in the records on location, kind of business, employment, payrolls, and business receipts gives a basis for an annual report that could be produced on a reasonably current basis for areas as small as counties.

The remaining 100,000 multi-unit companies present special problems because their components operate in a number of different industries, and the plants or business units may be in a number of different counties or even different states. By means of an annual survey, it will be possible to get the name, address, and industrial class of each component, together with information on employment, payrolls, and receipts. The mailing list thus obtained for the parts of the multi-unit firms would, when merged with the list for the remaining 7.9 million, furnish an across-the-board industrial directory. The responsibility for creating such a directory was given to the Census Bureau by an Office of Management and Budget directive issued in 1968.

Such an industrial directory is needed for the Census Bureau's own operations, as noted in Chapter X, and would be justified for that purpose alone. The directory would be important also for the use of other statistical agencies. Accordingly, legislative authority should be sought for sufficient modification of existing statutes to permit the transfer of directory-type information to other statistical agencies. With the precedent set by new legislation in Canada, it seems likely that Congress will approve this change.

When such a directory is authorized for use on a government-wide basis, there will be significant gains in both economy and efficiency. Savings will result because it will no longer be necessary to maintain duplicate directories in the various agencies that gather statistics from industrial firms. Efficiency will be improved when all censuses, surveys, and other inquiries are based on a common universe. Regardless of the extent to which the present decentralization of collection continues, the joint use of a common list will remove some of the existing uncertainties in the analysis of industrial data. When inconsistencies between different series occur, the use of ratio analysis on matched returns should make it possible for analysts to identify the cause of the differences. Study of the movements of labor cost per unit of output would be especially benefited by the use of a common directory for all inquiries.

In addition to providing a highly usable industrial directory, the combination of administrative records and the results of the annual surveys of the multi-unit firms would yield an important new series of annual data with reasonably current measures of economic activity classified by considerable industrial and geographical detail. Such a series would supplement the information in the County Business Patterns series (see Chapter V), which depends upon Social Security records and gives employment and first-quarter payrolls only. With the use of the address allocation facilities available in the Census Bureau, similar data could be prepared for special areas as needed, subject, of course, to nondisclosure requirements. An important feature of the new series is that the scope is not limited to activities that traditionally have been covered in the economic censuses. The opportunity to extend it to all fields of economic activity will provide for the first time bench-mark measures of some rapidly growing parts of the economy.

The traditional censuses of manufacturing, mining, trade, and services would be profoundly changed by the development of the new annual series. One of the traditional purposes of the censuses, the provision of local data on economic activity by industry, would be largely satisfied by the annual series based on administrative records.

The need for complete census coverage would have passed, and the traditional censuses could be based entirely on samples of establishments in the industrial directory. The data collected would be restricted in the main to kinds of information not contained in administrative records, such as merchandise and commodity lines, capacity and facilities, fuel and materials used, and classes of customers. The periodic censuses would be cheap enough compared to the old ones to cover much of the cost of the new directory and the annual series covering all establishments.

As reflected in the 1971 reorganization, the census of agriculture is more logically a part of the Bureau's economic program. With the continuing increase in the proportion of large farms and the reduction in the role of the traditional family farm, the demographic aspects of agriculture can be better covered through population surveys than through the census of agriculture. The new series of annual economic reports will cover agriculture, as reflected in the annual tax returns of farm operators. The periodic censuses of agriculture would then be directed toward information not provided in the tax returns, such as facilities, equipment, farming practices, and contractual arrangements.

Service Work

The production of statistics will continue to become more and more specialized, requiring an increasingly heavy investment in facilities and training. This is already evident in the development of more detailed maps, address lists, and directories, in the increased use of administrative records drawn from more than one source, in the advances in electronic equipment and techniques, and in the continued use of research to develop new ways of doing old tasks. The Census Bureau must continue to expand its capacity in all these directions, if its full potentialities as a service organization are to be realized.

Maps, National Address Lists, and Directories

The maps and address lists used for the 1970 census provide a good basis for the development of a national address register, suitable for all kinds of statistical inquiries. An early need is the development of a system of unique addresses in rural territory, which would furnish a truly national address register. With the address coding capability available with census facilities, such a register would give great flexibility in planning inquiries for areas tailored to meet very special needs. The use of this register of addresses, classified by information available from the census, would open the way to a stratified mailing list suitable for undertakings requiring predetermined proportions of different segments of the population. In exercising its responsibility for the management of this kind of resource, the Census Bureau will have to be alert to the danger of a new kind of pollution, that is, the pollution of the respondent universe, due to practices that alienate significant numbers of respondents.

With a national address register and an industrial directory, efficient mailings can be made to complete universes of citizens, establishments, or any kind of sample needed in a particular survey. The importance of the goal is great enough to justify fully a substantial commitment of equipment and human resources to make the system truly comprehensive and responsive to the requirements of all agencies within the confidentiality limitations imposed by law.

Equipment and Administrative Records

In the case of electronic equipment and associated software, the advantages for large-scale operations can be substantial. The largest computers not only offer the advantage of much greater operating speeds but also are free of some of the limitations that apply to smaller units. The Census Bureau pioneered in the application of the computer to data processing and should continue to provide the maximum statistical processing capability available within the federal statistical system. This capability is dependent not only on the size of the central computer but also on the variety and capacity of the peripheral equipment. For example, careful consideration should be given to the gains that might result from the acquisition of greatly enlarged memory systems. With greater memory capacity, it would be possible to store all the returns of any survey or census. Such a change would reduce the errors that now frequently arise in tape handling and open the way to greater processing flexibility.

In carrying out its regular tasks, the Census Bureau has already made impressive use of administrative records for both operating and statistical purposes. In the future, the Census Bureau should become a focal point, working in close consultation with the Office of Management and Budget in achieving maximum exploitation of such records. This may involve the presentation of data drawn solely from the administrative files or combined with other information in the Census files. In the former case, the agency having the files could, of course, prepare statistical summaries on its own initiative and, indeed, many have already done so. In all such cases, however, there is a danger that statistical uses will be subordinated to the operating requirements of the agency. In utilizing information drawn from separate sets of records, the Census Bureau would avoid the concern that has been expressed regarding the consolidation of records into a single data bank. The files would not be consolidated, no data could flow into the administrative agencies, and the responsibility for the maintenance of confidentiality would rest with the Census Bureau, which for many years has enjoyed the reputation of scrupulous protection of all information entrusted to it.

Research and Development

With the growing demand for factual information, coupled with increased competition for resources, the need for a substantial research and development program will increase.

Sampling will be useful in any effort to improve the supply of information without undue burden upon those from whom it must be obtained. Further work on the origins of error and the methods of reducing its size will make possible better service to users who want to know about the limitations of their data. Broad attention to the improvement of statistical design will help supply more precise knowledge about the dynamics of the American economy and the source of maladjustments. It may even prove possible through research to obtain some quantification of the supply and demand functions for statistics, thus substituting rational decision for what has been largely subjective judgment and intuition.

The Bureau should assume responsibility for some broad program planning to determine the kinds of statistical information that may be required in the light of substantial changes in economic organization and goals. A statistical service agency can serve best if it does not simply respond to requests from other agencies but also suggests the kinds of data and analyses that should become the concern of program agencies. In the achievement of these various objectives, it will be desirable to seek exchanges with the research staffs of other countries with similar economic problems. The exchange of experience will help bring faster progress in survey technology, in research and evaluation studies, and in planning for the future.

Organizational Changes

At the time this is being written, it appears that the work of the Census Bureau will not be greatly affected by the work of the President's Commission on Federal Statistics or by recent Departmental changes. The outlook for the future is promising whether the Census Bureau continues to function in the present Department of Commerce or becomes a part of a considerably larger Department of Economic Affairs—or of a central agency with the functions of coordination and statistical operations combined. The only indispensable ingredients in the appraisal are broad recognition of the importance of statistical work in the national scheme and acceptance of some degree of central responsibility to ensure that national goals receive greater emphasis than purely Departmental objectives.

Appendix A

Career Opportunities
in the Bureau of the Census

The size and variety of the tasks carried out by the Census Bureau provide attractive opportunities for those who consider making a career out of statistical work.* Because of the unique experience it furnishes in large scale operations of collection, processing, tabulation, and data delivery, many have chosen to work in the Bureau for a few years, even though their long-run interests are primarily in the field of analysis and interpretation. As a result, many statisticians and other professionals in government service have had a tour of duty in the Census Bureau early in their careers.

Kinds of Work

The present professional and management staff of more than 1,200 is comprised primarily of statisticians, economists,

---

* An interesting account of census work sixty years ago is presented in Francis Rolt-Wheeler's *Boy with the U.S. Census,* the story of Hamilton Noble, who started as an enumerator for the census of manufactures as a boy in Kentucky and later became an enumerator for the population census. He was transferred to the Washington office for card punching and later did field checking on defective returns.

221

sociologists, and program managers, but includes a broad representation of other fields. (See Table A-1.)

Some two-thirds of the professional staff are engaged in the field of statistics, concerned with the full range of procedures involved in modern methods of producing statistical information.

Typical assignments for the young statistician entering the Bureau upon graduation include doing background work for higher-level professionals, editing and assisting in testing schedules, and writing procedures and reports. Opportunities are very good for advancement to more difficult assignments such as designing questionnaires, developing procedures, analyzing statistical data, and assuming responsibility for specific steps in the census process. As an employee develops, a significant amount of his time is allocated to personal contacts with representatives of business and government to discuss general questions relating to the area of the nation's activity with which he is concerned. The prospects for advancement can be judged by the fact that the average Census Bureau statistician now reaches grade GS-12 in less than five years.

Mathematical statisticians, who represent about one-sixth of all statisticians, have quite specialized responsibility in over-all survey design and systems analysis. They assist in carrying out research in mathematical theory or related theoretical, analytical, or evaluation studies. They apply the principles of statistical inference and probability to the design of surveys in order to secure from samples the greatest amount of usable information. They develop or adapt methods for planning and executing statistical investigations, advise subject-matter specialists and applied statisticians on general plans for specific studies, analyze data for bias, and prepare final reports.

Professionals in the social sciences such as economics, sociology, and political science are usually concerned with

TABLE A-1

PERMANENT EMPLOYEES OF THE BUREAU OF THE CENSUS, AS OF MARCH, 1971, BY BROAD SERIES CLASSIFICATION AND GRADE LEVEL

Series Classification	Grades 1–2	Grades 3–9	Grades 10–15	Grades 16 and over	Total
Professional					
Statistical		227	633	10	870
Engineering		1	9		10
Computer		40	170		210
Other		14	39		53
Total Professional					1,143
Technical					
Computer		567	170		737
Informational & Editorial		21	30		51
Other		74	45		119
Total Technical					907
Operating					
Punch Card & Office Machines	19	287	10		316
Managerial					
Personnel		7	26		33
Accounting		13	61		74
Other		1	17	2	20
Total Managerial					127
Administrative and Clerical					
Secretarial-Typing	19	504			523
Supply & Procurement	1	37	4		42
Accounting & Payroll		33	5		38
Statistical, Clerical, etc.	27	997	53		1,077
Total Administrative and Clerical					1,680
Bureau Total	66	2,823	1,272	12	4,173

planning the output of subject-matter divisions in the form most helpful to users. In planning the content of censuses and surveys, they may have extensive contacts with both the suppliers and users of statistical data. Their specialized knowledge of particular subject fields makes them particularly useful in analysis and evaluation of results.

Because of its leadership in the development and use of automatic data processing systems, the Bureau offers especially good career opportunities in this expanding field. Each year the Bureau selects college graduates for assignments in data processing. New appointees receive several weeks of classroom instruction in computer programming techniques followed by approximately five months of on-the-job training as digital computer programmers. During this period they prepare sets of detailed instructions that specify the nature and sequence of computer actions and translate these into program or machine language acceptable to Bureau computers. As experience is acquired, new employees may develop new programming techniques.

Basic to the needs of the Bureau is the defining of the census tracts and other areas for which various census data are compiled and published. The Bureau's Geography Division is responsible for these aspects of the Bureau's over-all program and the geographers maintain constant contact with state and local governments in connection with those activities. The new college graduate who is appointed as a geographer will typically work on the development of a computerized system for coding addresses to geographical areas and on related activities, such as location-coding and longitude.

The increasing specialization of statistical work creates important opportunities for trained management analysts. Each year a limited number of college graduates are selected for assignment within the administrative service areas. For example, the graduate who comes in as an accountant will become part of one of the most modern accounting systems in government. Management analysts progress rapidly up the career ladder and are limited only by their own ability to apply imaginative thinking to the effective solution of management problems. Similarly, personnel management specialists, contract experts, and office services management specialists find rewarding careers in the Bureau.

CAREER DEVELOPMENT PROGRAMS

A variety of professional development programs and opportunities are available for new Bureau employees. These take the form of in-house lectures and seminars, courses outside the Bureau, and intern programs designed to speed up the readiness of employees to assume certain kinds of new assignments. Taken in combination, these various programs do much to close the knowledge gap between junior and senior members of the staff.

The Bureau has a full-time education director and draws on the services of senior professionals for instruction. The program makes use of study conferences on major aspects of the Bureau's programs and their relations to the federal establishment and the society at large and also utilizes group seminars, video-tape lectures, and reference materials.

With the passage of the Government Employees Training Act in 1958, the Bureau has been better able to encourage its professional employees to continue their professional training at educational institutions, in addition to attending governmental training courses. In illustration of the level of activity, more than 300 employees took courses at local colleges and universities in a recent year, and another 240 took part in interagency programs within the government. As the employees progress up the career ladder, middle management training courses designed to give greater ability in management skills are available periodically, including courses in human relations and delegation of authority. Similarly, as dictated by the needs of the Bureau, special executive development programs are available to those regarded as potential executives.

A number of intern programs provide a basis for speeding up the development of outstanding junior and middle-level professionals and management staff members by furnishing them, on a rotating basis, with a variety of developmental experiences. The results of such programs in both professional and managerial fields indicate that properly selected individuals, given a chance to broaden their experience in a planned program, usually qualify quite rapidly for advancement.

A good deal of career development results simply from the contacts available in the Bureau. As a member of the professional staff of the Bureau, the young graduate will establish associations with many outstanding specialists who enjoy national and international reputations in professional circles. Contacts with senior employees will expose new workers to the excitement that can come from finding better ways to do old tasks. New ideas and innovative approaches are often contributed by new workers as well as by older ones. New employees are encouraged to participate in the activities of professional organizations. The American Association for the Advancement of Science and twenty-four other professional organizations count Bureau employees among their members.

APPLICATION PROCEDURES

Recent graduates or college seniors who are interested in applying for professional or management type positions with the Bureau of the Census are asked to complete a Personal Qualifications Statement (SF-171) form and forward it to the College Relations Officer, Bureau of the Census, Washington, D.C., with a list of all college courses and grades. For the recent college graduate, most computer programmer, management analyst, and economist appointments are made through the Civil Service Commission's Federal Service Entrance Examination. For all statistician positions, appointments for the recent college graduate are through the Civil Service Commission's Engineer Scientists and Related Professionals Examination. Appointments in such cases are made at the GS-5 or GS-7 level, depending on the ratings in the examination. For those with master degrees a higher level may be available.

Experienced applicants applying for positions at the GS-9 level and higher are asked to complete a Personal Qualifications Statement (SF-171) as well as Form SF-226 (Course Listing) and forward them to the Employment Officer, Bureau of the Census, Washington, D.C., 20233. Appointments at such levels for statisticians, including the mathematical statisticians, are made through the Civil Service Commission's Science and Engineering Examination. Computer programmer appointments are made through the Civil Service Commission's Computer Specialists Examination. Administrative and management type appointments at the GS-9 through GS-12 level are made through the Civil Service Commission's Mid-Level Positions Examination. Such appointments at the GS-13 level through GS-15 level are made through the Civil Service Commission's Senior Level Positions Examination.

Appendix B

Directors of the Bureau
of the Census, 1902-72

Department of the Interior (1902–3)

    William Rush Merriam   1902 –

Department of Commerce and Labor (1903–13)

William Rush Merriam	– 1903
Simon Newton Dexter North	1903 – 1909
Edward Dana Durand	1909 – 1913

Department of Commerce (March 1913 to date)

William Julius Harris	1913 – 1915
Sam Lyle Rogers	1915 – 1921
William Mott Steuart	1921 – 1933
William Lane Austin	1933 – 1941
Vergil Daniel Reed (acting director)	Feb. 1941 – May 1941
James Clyde Capt	1941 – 1949
Philip Morris Hauser (acting director)	Aug. 1949 – March 1950
Roy Victor Peel	1950 – 1953
Robert Wilbur Burgess	1953 – 1961

Albert Ross Eckler (acting director)	March 1961 – May 1961
Richard Montgomery Scammon	1961 – 1965
Albert Ross Eckler	1965 – 1969
George Hay Brown	Sept. 1969 –

Appendix C

Population and Housing Census Questions, 1790–1970

1790

Name of family head; free white males of sixteen years and up, free white males under sixteen; free white females; slaves; other persons.

1800

Name of family head; if white, age and sex; race; slaves.

1810

Name of family head; if white, age and sex; race; slaves.

1820

Name of family head; age; sex; race; foreigners not naturalized; slaves; industry (agriculture, commerce, and manufactures).

1830

Name of family head; age; sex; race; slaves; deaf and dumb; blind; foreigners not naturalized.

1840

Name of family head; age; sex; race; slaves; number of deaf and dumb; number of blind; number of insane and idiotic and whether in public or private charge; number of persons in each family employed in each of six classes of industry and one of occupation; literacy; pensioners for Revolutionary or military service.

1850

Name; age; sex; race; whether deaf and dumb, blind, insane, or idiotic; value of real estate; occupation; birthplace; whether married within the year; school attendance; literacy; whether a pauper or convict.

Supplemental schedules for slaves; public paupers and criminals; persons who died during the year.

1860

Name; age; sex; race; value of real estate; value of personal estate; occupation; birthplace; whether married within the year; school attendance; literacy; whether deaf and dumb, blind, insane, idiotic, pauper, or convict; number of slave houses.

Supplemental schedules for slaves; public paupers and criminals; persons who died during the year.

1870

Name; age; sex, race; occupation; value of real estate; value of personal estate; birthplace; whether parents were foreign born; month of birth if born within the year; month of marriage if married within the year; school attendance; literacy; whether deaf and dumb, blind, insane or idiotic; male citizens twenty-one and over, and number of such persons denied the right to vote for other than rebellion.

Supplemental schedules for persons who died during the year; paupers; prisoners.

1880

Address; name; relationship to family head; sex; race; age; marital status; month of birth if born within the census year; married within the year; occupation; months unemployed during the year; sickness or temporary disability; whether blind, deaf and dumb, idiotic, insane, maimed, crippled, bedridden, or otherwise disabled; school attendance; literacy; birthplace of person and parents.

Supplemental schedules for the Indian population; for persons who died during the year; insane; idiots; deaf-mutes; blind; homeless children; prisoners; paupers and indigent persons.

1890

Address; number of families in house; number of persons in house; number of persons in family; name; whether a soldier, sailor, or marine during Civil War (Union or Confederate) or widow of such person; relationship to family head; race; sex; age; marital status; whether married during census year; for women, number of children born and number now living; birthplace of person and parents; if foreign born, number of years in the U.S., whether naturalized or whether naturalization papers had been taken out; profession, trade, or occupation; months unemployed during year; school attendance; literacy; whether able to speak English, and if not, language or dialect spoken; whether suffering from acute or chronic disease, with name of disease and length of time afflicted; whether defective in mind, sight, hearing, or speech, or whether crippled, maimed, or deformed, with name of defect; whether a prisoner, convict, homeless child, or pauper; home owned or rented, and if owned, whether mortgaged; if family head a farmer, whether farm rented or owned, and if owned, whether mortgaged.

Supplemental schedules for the Indian population; for persons who died during the year; insane; feeble-minded and idiots; deaf; blind; diseased and physically defective; inmates of benevolent institutions; prisoners; paupers and indigent persons; surviving soldiers, sailors, and marines, and widows of such; inmates of soldiers' homes; for owner-occupied mortgaged houses.

1900

Address; name; relationship to family head; sex; race; age; marital status; number of years married; for women, number of children born and number now living; birthplace of person and parents; if foreign born, year of immigration, and whether naturalized; occupation; months not employed; school attendance; literacy; ability to speak English; whether on a farm; home owned or rented; if owned, whether mortgaged.

Supplemental schedules for the blind and for the deaf.

1910

Address; name; relationship to family head; sex; race; age; marital status; number of years of present marriage; for women, number of children born and number now living; birthplace and mother tongue of person and parents; if foreign born, year of immigration, whether naturalized, and whether able to speak English, or if not, language spoken; occupation, industry, and class of worker; if an employee, whether out of work on census day and weeks out of work during year; literacy; school attendance; home owned or rented; if owned, whether mortgaged; whether farm or house; whether a survivor of Union or Confederate Army or Navy; whether blind or deaf and dumb.

Supplemental schedules for the Indian population; blind;

deaf; feeble-minded in institutions; insane in hospitals; paupers in almshouse; prisoners and juvenile delinquents in institutions.

1920

Address; name; relationship to family head; sex; race; age; marital status; if foreign born, year of immigration to the U.S., whether naturalized, and year of naturalization; school attendance; literacy; birthplace of person and parents; mother tongue of foreign born; ability to speak English; occupation, industry, and class of worker; home owned or rented; if owned, whether mortgaged; for nonfarm mortgaged, market value, original amount of mortgage, balance due, interest rate.

Supplemental schedules for the blind and for the deaf.

1930

Address; name; relationship to family head; home owned or rented; value or monthly rental; radio set; whether on a farm; sex; race; age; marital status; age at first marriage; school attendance; literacy; birthplace of person and parents; if foreign born, language spoken in home before coming to U.S., year of immigration, whether naturalized, and ability to speak English; occupation, industry, and class of worker; whether at work previous day (or last regular working day); veteran status; for Indians, whether of full or mixed blood, and tribal affiliation.

Supplemental schedules for gainful workers not at work on the day preceding the enumeration; blind and deaf-mutes.

1940

POPULATION

Information obtained for all persons: Address; home owned or rented; value or monthly rental; whether on a farm; name;

relationship to household head; sex; race; age; marital status; school attendance; educational attainment; birthplace; citizenship of foreign born; location of residence five years ago and whether on a farm; employment status; if at work, whether in private or nonemergency government work, or in public emergency work (WPA, CCC, NYA, etc.); if in private or nonemergency government work, hours worked in week; if seeking work or on public emergency work, duration of unemployment; occupation, industry, and class of worker; weeks worked last year; income last year.

Information for 5 per cent sample: Birthplace of parents; language spoken in home in earliest childhood; veteran status; whether wife or widow of veteran; whether child of veteran and, if so, whether father living; whether has Social Security number and whether deductions were made from all or part of wages or salary; occupation, industry, and class of worker; for women ever married, whether married more than once, age at first marriage, and number of children ever born.

Supplemental schedule for infants born during the four months preceding the census.

HOUSING

Information obtained for all housing units: Occupied or vacant; owned or rented; value or rent; if owned, whether mortgaged; if vacant, year-round or seasonal, and vacancy status; type of structure; number of rooms; year built; original purpose of building; exterior material; number of units in structure; condition; water supply; toilet facilities; bathing facilities; lighting; heating equipment; heating fuel; cooking fuel; refrigeration; radio set; for nonfarm renter-occupied, gross rent, and, if furnished, estimated rent unfurnished; for nonfarm owner-occupied, estimated rent, and, if mortgaged, balance due, interest rate, type of mortgage holder, distribution and amount of mortgage payments.

NOTE: All inquiries in the 1790 through 1930 censuses were asked for all applicable persons.

There were no housing censuses conducted prior to 1940. A few housing inquiries were included in the decennial population censuses in 1860 and 1890–1930.

1950

POPULATION

Information obtained for all persons: Address; whether house is on farm; name; relationship to household head; race; sex; age; marital status; birthplace; if foreign born, whether naturalized; employment status; hours worked in week; occupation, industry, and class of worker.

Information obtained for 20 per cent sample: Whether living in same house a year ago; whether living on a farm a year ago; location of residence a year ago; country of birth of parents; educational attainment; school attendance; if looking for work, number of weeks; weeks worked last year; income last year; veteran status.

Information obtained for 3⅓ per cent sample: For persons who worked last year but not in current labor force: Occupation, industry, and class of worker on last job; if ever married, whether married more than once; duration of present marital status; for women ever married, number of children ever born.

Supplemental schedules for persons on Indian reservations; infants born in the first three months of 1950; Americans overseas.

HOUSING

Information obtained for all housing units: Occupied or vacant; owned or rented; if vacant, whether year-round or seasonal; type of living quarters; type of structure; number of rooms; year built; number of units in structure; condition; water supply; toilet facilities; bathing facilities.

Information obtained for all nonfarm housing units: If owned, whether mortgaged, market value; if vacant, monthly rental or sale price; if rented, contract rent, gross rent, and, if furnished, estimated rent unfurnished.

Information obtained for 20 per cent sample: Lighting; heating equipment; heating fuel; cooking fuel; refrigeration; kitchen sink; radio set; television set.

Supplemental schedules for Indians and residential finance.

1960

POPULATION

Information obtained for all persons: Address; name; relationship to household head; sex; race; age; marital status.

Information obtained for 25 per cent sample: Birthplace, if foreign born, language spoken in home before coming to U.S.; country of birth of parents; length of residence at present address; location of residence five years ago; educational attainment; school attendance; whether married more than once and date of first marriage; for women ever married, number of children ever born; employment status; hours worked in week; year last worked; occupation, industry, and class of worker; location of place of work; means of transportation to work; weeks worked last year; income last year; veteran status.

Supplemental schedule for Americans overseas.

HOUSING

Information obtained for all housing units: Occupied or vacant, owned, rented, or no cash rent; if vacant, year-round, seasonal, or migratory, and vacancy status; trailers; number of rooms; access to unit; condition; water supply; toilet facilities; bathing facilities; kitchen, cooking facilities; value or contract rent (obtained for all housing units in large cities and for a 25 per cent sample elsewhere).

Information obtained for 25 per cent sample: Whether on a farm; duration of vacancy; year built; if trailer, whether mobile or fixed; heating equipment; telephone available; gross rent.

Information obtained for 20 per cent sample: Number of units in structure; basement; elevator (obtained only in large cities); number of bathrooms; source of water (obtained only outside large cities); sewage disposal (obtained only outside large cities); automobiles (in large cities; elsewhere obtained for a 5 per cent sample).

Information obtained for 5 per cent sample: Number of bedrooms; heating fuel; cooking fuel; water heating fuel; radio sets; clothes washing machines; clothes dryers; home food freezers; air conditioning; television sets.

Supplemental schedules for components of housing inventory change and for residential finance.

1970

POPULATION

Information obtained for all persons: Address; name; relationship to household head; sex; race; age; marital status.

Information obtained for 20 per cent sample: Birthplace; educational attainment; for women, number of children ever born; employment status; hours worked in week; year last worked; occupation, industry, and class of worker; activity five years ago, weeks worked last year; income last year; location of residence five years ago.

Information obtained for 15 per cent sample: Country of birth of parents; length of residence at present address; language spoken in childhood home; school attendance; veteran status; location of place of work; means of transportation to work.

Information obtained for 5 per cent sample: If foreign born, whether naturalized, and year of immigration; whether married more than once, date of first marriage, and whether first marriage ended because of death of spouse; vocational training; for persons of working age, presence and duration of disability; occupation, industry, and class of worker five years ago.

HOUSING

Information obtained for all housing units: Occupied or vacant; owned, rented, or no cash rent; if vacant, vacancy status (for sale, for rent, etc.) and duration of vacancy; number of units at this address; single or multiple family structure; trailers; number of rooms; basement; access to unit; water supply; toilet facilities; bathing facilities; kitchen facilities; telephone available; value or contract rent.

Information obtained for 20 per cent sample: Whether on a farm; year built; number of units in structure; gross rent; heating equipment.

Information obtained for 15 per cent sample: Number of bathrooms; source of water; sewage disposal; air conditioning; automobiles.

Information obtained for 5 per cent sample: Number of bedrooms; number of stories; elevators; heating fuel; cooking fuel; water heating fuel; battery-operated radio sets; clothes washing machines; clothes dryers; home food freezers; television sets; dishwashers; second homes.

Appendix D

Title 13, United States Code—Census

CONTENTS

* Codification of August 1954, amended by acts of August, 1957, September, 1960, June and October, 1962, and August, 1964. The less important sections have been omitted.

Offenses and Penalties
    Officers and Employees
    Other Persons
Collection and Publication of Foreign Commerce
    and Trade Statistics

ADMINISTRATION

General Provisions

§ 2. *Bureau of the Census*

The Bureau is continued as an agency within, and under the jurisdiction of, the Department of Commerce.

§ 4. *Functions of Secretary; delegation*

The Secretary [of Commerce] shall perform the functions and duties imposed upon him by this title or he may delegate any of them to such officers, employees, bureaus or agencies of the Department of Commerce as he designates.

§ 5. *Schedules; number, form, and scope of inquiries*

The Secretary shall prepare schedules, and shall determine the inquiries, and the number, form, and subdivisions thereof, for the statistics, surveys, and censuses provided for in this title.

§ 6. *Requests to other departments and offices for information, acquisition of reports from governmental and other sources*

(a) The Secretary, whenever he deems it advisable, may call upon any other department or office of the Government for information pertinent to the work provided for in this title.

(b) The Secretary may acquire by purchase, or otherwise from States, counties, cities, or other units of government, or their instrumentalities, or from private persons and agencies such copies of records, reports, and other material as may be required for the efficient and economical conduct of the censuses and surveys provided for in this title.

§ 8. *Certified copies of certain returns; other data; restriction on use; disposition of fees received*

(a) The Secretary may, upon a written request, and in his discretion, furnish to Governors of States and Territories, courts of record, and individuals, data for genealogical and other proper purposes, from the population, agriculture, and housing schedules prepared under the authority of subchapter II of chapter 5, upon the payment of the actual, or estimated cost of searching the records and $1 for supplying a certificate.

(b) The Secretary may furnish transcripts or copies of tables and other census records and make special statistical compilations and surveys for State or local officials, private concerns, or individuals upon the payment of the actual, or estimated cost of such work. In the case of nonprofit organizations or agencies the Secretary may engage in joint statistical projects, the cost of which shall be shared equitably as determined by the Secretary and provided that the purposes are otherwise authorized by law.

(c) In no case shall information furnished under the authority of this section be used to the detriment of the persons to whom such information relates.

(d) All moneys received in payment for work or services enumerated under this section shall be deposited in a separate account which may be used to pay directly the costs of such work or services, to repay appropriations which initially bore all or part of such costs, or to refund excess sums when necessary.

§ 9. *Information as confidential; exception*

(a) Neither the Secretary, nor any other officer or employee of the Department of Commerce or bureau or agency thereof, may, except as provided in section 8 of this title—

(1) use the information furnished under the provisions of this title for any purpose other than the statistical purposes for which it is supplied; or

(2) make any publication whereby the data furnished by any particular establishment or individual under this title can be identified; or

(3) permit anyone other than the sworn officers and employees of the Department or bureau or agency thereof to examine the individual reports.

No department, bureau, agency, officer, or employee of the Government, except the Secretary in carrying out the purposes of this title, shall require, for any reason, copies of census reports which have been retained by any such establishment or individual. Copies of census reports which have been so retained shall be immune from legal process, and shall not, without the consent of the individual or establishment concerned, be admitted as evidence or used for any purpose in any action, suit, or other judicial or administrative proceeding.

(b) The provisions of subsection (a) of this section relating to the confidential treatment of data for particular individuals and establishments, shall not apply to the censuses of governments provided for by subchapter III of chapter 5 of this title, nor to interim current data provided for by subchapter IV of chapter 5 of this title as to the subjects covered by censuses of governments, with respect to any information obtained therefor that is compiled from, or customarily provided in, public records.

Officers and Employees

§ 21. *Director of the Census; duties*

The Bureau shall be headed by a Director of the Census, appointed by the President, by and with the advice and consent of the Senate. The Director shall perform such duties as may be imposed upon him by law, regulations, or orders of the Secretary.

§ 23. *Additional officers and employees*

(a) The Secretary may establish, at rates of compensation to be fixed by him without regard to the Classification Act of 1949, as many temporary positions as may be necessary to meet the requirements of the work provided for by law. Bureau employees who are transferred to any such temporary positions shall not lose their permanent civil service status by reason of the transfer. The Secretary may make appointments to such temporary positions in conformity with the civil service laws and rules.

(b) In addition to employees of the Department of Commerce, employees of other departments and independent offices of the Government may, with the consent of the head of the respective department or office, be employed and compensated for field work in connection with the work provided for by law without regard to section 301 of the Dual Compensation Act.

§ 24. *Special employment provisions*

(a) The Secretary may utilize the service of nontemporary employees of the Bureau (by assignment, promotion, appointment, detail, or otherwise) in temporary positions established for any census, for not to exceed the period during which appropriations are available for that census. Whenever the Secretary determines that the services of an employee which have been utilized under this section are no longer required in such a temporary position, he may, without regard to the provisions of any other law, return the employee to a continuing position, with rank and compensation not less than that which he held in his last permanent position in the Bureau: *Provided*, That no employee shall, by reason of his service in a temporary position under this subsection, lose the protection of any law or regulation with respect to his separation, suspension, furlough, or reduction in rank or compensation below the level held in his last permanent position in the Bureau. Service by a nontemporary employee in a temporary position under this subsection shall be creditable for step-increases (both periodic and longevity) under title VII of the Classification Act of 1949, as amended, as though it were a continuation of service in his last permanent position.

(b) As used in this title with respect to appointments or positions, 'temporary' shall be construed to mean not in excess of one year, or not in excess of the specific period during which appropriations are available for the conduct of a particular census, whichever is longer. No employee of the Bureau who holds only a temporary appointment within the meaning of this section shall be considered as other than strictly temporary for purposes of any other provision of law relating to separations, suspensions, or reductions in rank or compensation.

(c) The enlisted men and officers of the uniformed services may be appointed and compensated for service in temporary enumerator positions for the enumeration of personnel of the uniformed services.

(d) The Secretary may fix compensation on a piece-price basis without limitations as to the amount earned per diem, and payments may be made to enumerators for the use of private automobiles on official business without regard to section 4 of the Travel Expense Act of 1949, as amended (5 U.S.C. 837), but at rates not in excess of the rates provided by that Act.

(e) The Secretary may authorize the expenditure of necessary sums for travel expenses of persons selected for appointment for attendance at training courses held by the Department of Commerce with respect to any of the work provided for by law.

(f) Notwithstanding any other provision of law prohibiting the expenditure of public money for telephone service, the

Secretary, under such regulations as he shall prescribe, may authorize reimbursement for tolls or charges for telephone service from private residences or private apartments to the extent such charges are determined by the Secretary to have been incurred to facilitate the collection of information in connection with the censuses and surveys authorized by this title.

COLLECTION AND PUBLICATION OF STATISTICS

Cotton

§ 41. *Collection and publication*

The Secretary shall collect and publish statistics concerning the—

(1) amount of cotton ginned;
(2) quantity of raw cotton consumed in manufacturing establishments of every character;
(3) quantity of baled cotton on hand;
(4) number of active consuming cotton spindles;
(5) number of active spindle hours; and
(6) quantity of cotton imported and exported, with the country of origin and destination.

§ 45. *Simultaneous publication of cotton reports*

The reports of cotton ginned to the dates as of which the Department of Agriculture is also required to issue cotton crop reports shall be issued simultaneously with the cotton crop reports of that department, the two reports to be issued from the same place at 11 o'clock antemeridian on the eighth day following that on which the respective reports relate. When such date of release falls on Sunday, a legal holiday, or other day which pursuant to statute or Executive Order is a nonworkday in the Department of Commerce at Washington generally, the reports shall be issued at 11 o'clock antemeridian of the next succeeding workday.

Miscellaneous

§ 101. *Defective, dependent, and delinquent classes; crime*
(a) The Secretary may collect decennially statistics relating—

> (1) to the defective, dependent, and delinquent classes; and
> (2) to crime, including judicial statistics pertaining thereto.

(b) The statistics authorized by subsection (a) of this section shall include information upon the following questions, namely: age, sex, color, nativity, parentage, literacy by race, color, nativity, and parentage, and such other questions relating to such subjects as the Secretary deems proper.

(c) In addition to the decennial collections authorized by subsections (a) and (b) of this section, the Secretary may compile and publish annually statistics relating to crime and to the defective, dependent, and delinquent classes.

§ 102. *Religion*
The Secretary may collect decennially statistics relating to religious bodies.

§ 103. *Designation of reports*
All reports covering any of the statistics collected under the provisions of this subchapter shall be designated as "Special Reports" followed by the name of whatever bureau or agency of the Department of Commerce is designated by the Secretary to collect and compile such statistics.

CENSUSES

Manufactures, Mineral Industries, and Other Businesses

§ 131. *Collection and publication; five-year periods*
The Secretary shall take, compile, and publish censuses of

manufactures, of mineral industries, and of other businesses, including the distributive trades, service establishments, and transportation (exclusive of means of transportation for which statistics are required by law to be filed with, and are compiled and published by, a designated regulatory body), in the year 1964, then in the year 1968, and every fifth year thereafter, and each such census shall relate to the year immediately preceding the taking thereof.

Population, Housing, Agriculture, Irrigation, Drainage, and Unemployment

§ 141. *Population, unemployment, and housing*

(a) The Secretary shall, in the year 1960 and every ten years thereafter, take a census of population, unemployment, and housing (including utilities and equipment) as of the first day of April, which shall be known as the census date.

(b) The tabulation of total population by States as required for the apportionment of Representatives shall be completed within eight months of the census date and reported by the Secretary to the President of the United States.

§ 142. *Agriculture, irrigation, and drainage*

(a) The Secretary shall, beginning in the month of October 1959, and in the same month of every fifth year thereafter, take a census of agriculture, provided that the censuses directed to be taken in October 1959 and each tenth year thereafter, may, when and where deemed advisable by the Secretary, be taken instead in conjunction with the censuses provided in section 141 of this title.

(b) The Secretary shall, in conjunction with the census of agriculture directed to be taken in October 1959 and each tenth year thereafter, take a census of irrigation and drainage.

Governments

§ 161. *Quinquennial censuses; inclusion of certain data*

The Secretary shall take, compile, and publish for the year

1957 and for every fifth year thereafter a census of governments. Each such census shall include, but shall not be limited to, data on taxes and tax valuations, governmental receipts, expenditures, indebtedness, and employees of States, counties, cities, and other governmental units.

§ 163. *Authority of other agencies*

This subchapter does not revoke or impair the authority of any other Federal agency with respect to the collection or release of information.

Interim Current Data

§ 181. *Surveys*

The Secretary may make surveys deemed necessary to furnish annual and other interim current data on the subjects covered by the censuses provided for in this title.

Geographic Scope, Preliminary and Supplemental Statistics, and Use of Sampling

§ 191. *Geographic scope of censuses*

(a) Each of the censuses authorized by this chapter (other than censuses of population) shall include each State, the District of Columbia, Alaska, Hawaii, the Virgin Islands, Guam, and the Commonwealth of Puerto Rico, and as may be determined by the Secretary, such other possessions and areas over which the United States exercises jurisdiction, control, or sovereignty. Censuses of population shall include all geographic areas referred to in the preceding sentence. Inclusion of other areas over which the United States exercises jurisdiction or control shall be subject to the concurrence of the Secretary of State.

(b) For censuses taken in the Virgin Islands, Guam, or any possession or area not specifically designated in (a) above, the Secretary may utilize or adopt census data collected by the Governor or highest ranking Federal official, when such data are obtained in accordance with plans prescribed or approved by the Secretary.

(c) When, under determination by the Secretary as provided in paragraph (a) above, any census is not taken in a possession or area over which the United States exercises jurisdiction, control, or sovereignty, the Secretary may include in the census report data obtained from other Federal agencies or Government sources. Any data obtained from foreign governments shall be obtained through the Secretary of State.

§ 193. *Preliminary and supplemental statistics*

In advance of, in conjunction with, or after the taking of each census provided for by this chapter, the Secretary may make surveys and collect such preliminary and supplementary statistics related to the main topic of the census as are necessary to the initiation, taking, or completion thereof.

§ 195. *Use of sampling*

Except for the determination of population for apportionment purposes, the Secretary may, where he deems it appropriate, authorize the use of the statistical method known as "sampling" in carrying out the provisions of this title.

OFFENSES AND PENALTIES

Officers and Employees

§ 214. *Wrongful disclosure of information*

Whoever, being an employee referred to in subchapter II of chapter 1 of this title, having taken and subscribed the oath of office, publishes or communicates, without the written authority of the Secretary or other authorized officer or employee of the Department of Commerce or bureau or agency thereof, any information coming into his possession by reason of his employment under the provisions of this title, shall be fined not more than $1,000 or imprisoned not more than two years, or both.

Other Persons

§ 221. *Refusal or neglect to answer questions; false answers*

(a) Whoever, being over eighteen years of age, refuses or willfully neglects, when requested by the Secretary, or by any other authorized officer or employee of the Department of Commerce or bureau or agency thereof acting under the instructions of the Secretary or authorized officer, to answer, to the best of his knowledge, any of the questions on any schedule submitted to him in connection with any census or survey provided for by subchapters I, II, IV, and V of chapter 5 of this title, applying to himself or to the family to which he belongs or is related, or to the farm or farms of which he or his family is the occupant, shall be fined not more than $100 or imprisoned not more than sixty days, or both.

(b) Whoever, when answering questions described in subsection (a) of this section, and under the conditions or circumstances described in such subsection, willfully gives any answer that is false, shall be fined not more than $500 or imprisoned not more than one year, or both.

§ 222. *Giving suggestions or information with intent to cause inaccurate enumeration of population*

Whoever, either directly or indirectly, offers or renders to any officer or employee of the Department of Commerce or bureau or agency thereof engaged in making an enumeration of population under subchapter II, IV, or V of chapter 5 of this title, any suggestion, advice, information or assistance of any kind, with the intent or purpose of causing an inaccurate enumeration of population to be made, shall be fined not more than $1,000 or imprisoned not more than one year, or both.

§ 223. *Refusal, by owners, proprietors, etc., to assist census employees*

Whoever, being the owner, proprietor, manager, superintendent, or agent of any hotel, apartment house, boarding or lodging house, tenement, or other building, refuses, or willfully neglects, when requested by the Secretary or by any other officer or employee of the Department of Commerce or bureau or agency thereof, acting under the instructions of the Secretary, to furnish the names of the occupants of such premises, or to give free ingress thereto and egress therefrom to any duly accredited representative of such Department or bureau or agency thereof, so as to permit the collection of statistics with respect to any census provided for in subchapters I and II of chapter 5 of this title, or any survey authorized by subchapter IV or V of such chapter in so far as such survey relates to any of the subjects for which censuses are provided by such subchapters I and II, including, when relevant to the census or survey being taken or made, the proper and correct enumeration of all persons having their usual place of abode in such premises, shall be fined not more than $500.

§ 224. *Failure to answer questions affecting companies, businesses, religious bodies, and other organizations; false answers*

Whoever, being the owner, official, agent, person in charge, or assistant to the person in charge, of any company, business, institution, establishment, religious body, or organization of any nature whatsoever, neglects or refuses, when requested by the Secretary or other authorized officer or employee of the Department of Commerce or bureau or agency thereof, whether such request be made by registered mail, by certified mail, by telegraph, by visiting representative, or by one or more of these methods, to answer completely and correctly to the best of his knowledge all questions relating to his company, business, institution, establishment, religious body, or other organization, or to records or statistics in his official custody, contained on any census or other schedule prepared and submitted to him under the authority of this title, shall be fined not more than $500 or imprisoned not more than sixty days, or both; and if he willfully gives a false answer to any such question, he shall be fined not more than $10,000 or imprisoned not more than one year, or both.

§ 225. *Applicability of penal provisions in certain cases*

(a) In connection with any survey conducted by the Secretary or other authorized officer or employee of the Department of Commerce or Bureau or agency thereof pursuant to subchapter IV of chapter 5 of this title, the provisions of sections 221, 222, 223, and 224 of this title shall apply—

(1) with respect to the answering of questions and furnishing of information, only to such inquiries as are within the scope of the schedules and of the type and character heretofore used in connection with the taking of complete censuses under subchapters I and II of chapter 5 of this title, or in connection with any censuses hereafter taken pursuant to such subchapters;

(2) only after publication of a determination with reasons therefor certified by the Secretary, or by some other authorized officer or employee of the Department of Commerce or bureau or agency thereof with the approval of the Secretary, that the information called for is needed to aid or permit the efficient performance of essential governmental functions or services, or has significant application to the needs of the public, business, or industry and is not publicly available from nongovernmental or other governmental sources;

(3) in the case of any new survey, only after public notice, given by the Secretary or other authorized officer or employee of the Department of Commerce or bureau or agency thereof at least thirty days in advance of requesting a return, that such survey is under consideration.

(b) The provisions for imprisonment provided by sections

221, 222, and 224 of this title shall not apply in connection with any survey conducted pursuant to subchapter II of chapter 3 of this title, or to subchapter IV of chapter 5 of this title.

(c) The provisions of sections 221, 222, 223, and 224 of this title shall not apply to any censuses or surveys of governments provided for by subchapters III and IV of chapter 5 of this title, nor to other surveys provided for by subchapter IV of such chapter which are taken more frequently than annually.

(d) Where the doctrine, teaching, or discipline of any religious denomination or church prohibits the disclosure of information relative to membership, a refusal, in such circumstances, to furnish such information shall not be an offense under this chapter.

COLLECTION AND PUBLICATION OF FOREIGN COMMERCE AND TRADE STATISTICS

§ 301. *Collection and publication*

The Secretary is authorized to collect information from all persons exporting from, or importing into, the United States and the noncontiguous areas over which the United States exercises sovereignty, jurisdiction, or control, and from all persons engaged in trade between the United States and such noncontiguous areas and between those areas, or from the owners, or operators of carriers engaged in such foreign commerce or trade, and shall compile and publish such information pertaining to exports, imports, trade, and transportation relating thereto, as he deems necessary or appropriate to enable him to foster, promote, develop, and further the commerce, domestic and foreign, of the United States and for other lawful purposes.

§ 302. *Rules, regulations, and orders*

The Secretary may make such rules, regulations, and orders

as he deems necessary or appropriate to carry out the provisions of this chapter. Any rules, regulations, or orders issued pursuant to this authority may be established in such form or manner, may contain such classifications or differentiations, and may provide for such adjustments and reasonable exceptions as in the judgment of the Secretary are necessary or proper to effectuate the purpose of this chapter, or to prevent circumvention or evasion of any rule, regulation, or order issued hereunder. The Secretary may also provide by rule or regulation, for such confidentiality, publication, or disclosure, of information collected hereunder as he may deem necessary or appropriate in the public interest. Rules, regulations, and orders, or amendments thereto shall have the concurrence of the Secretary of the Treasury prior to promulgation.

§ 305. *Violations, penalties*

Any person, including the owners or operators of carriers, violating the provisions of this chapter, or any rule, regulation, or order issued thereunder, except as provided in section 304 above, shall be liable to a penalty not to exceed $1,000 in addition to any other penalty imposed by law. The amount of any such penalty shall be payable into the Treasury of the United States and shall be recoverable in a civil suit in the name of the United States.

§ 306. *Delegation of Functions*

Subject to the concurrence of the head of the department or agency concerned, the Secretary may make such provisions as he shall deem appropriate, authorizing the performance by any officer, agency, or employee of the United States Government departments or offices, or the governments of any areas over which the United States exercises sovereignty, jurisdiction, or control, of any function of the Secretary, contained in this chapter.

Bibliography

BOOKS

ALTERMAN, HYMAN. *Counting People: The Census in History.* New York: Harcourt, 1969.

American Economic Association. *The Federal Census.* Critical Essays by members of the Association. New York, 1899.

FISHER, RONALD A. *The Design of Experiments.* London: Oliver and Boyd, 1935; 8th ed., New York: Hafner, 1966.

HANSEN, MORRIS H., WILLIAM N. HURWITZ, and WILLIAM G. MADOW. *Sample Survey Methods and Theory.* Vol. I, *Methods and Applications;* Vol. II, *Theory.* New York: Wiley, 1953.

HAUSER, PHILIP M., and WILLIAM R. LEONARD (eds.). *Government Statistics for Business Use.* New York: Wiley, 1956.

HOLT, W. STULL. *The Bureau of the Census.* Washington: Brookings Institution, 1929.

KOREN, JOHN. *The History of Statistics: Their Development and Progress in Many Countries.* New York: Macmillan, 1918.

MILLS, FREDERICK C., and CLARENCE D. LONG. *The Statistical Agencies of the Federal Government.* New York: National Bureau of Economic Research, 1949.

MORTON, J. E. *On the Evolution of Manpower Statistics.* Washington: Upjohn Institute for Employment Research, 1969.

National Planning Association. *Technical Cooperation in Latin America.* Washington, 1957.

RICE, STUART A., et al. *Next Steps in the Development of Social Statistics.* Ann Arbor: Edwards Brothers, 1933.

ROLT-WHEELER, FRANCIS. *The Boy with the U.S. Census.* Boston: Lothrop, Lee and Shepard, 1911.

SCHLESINGER, ARTHUR M. *New Viewpoints in American History.* New York: Macmillan, 1926.

SCHMECKEBIER, LAURENCE F. *Congressional Apportionment.* Washington: Brookings Institution, 1941.

SCOTT, ANN HERBERT. *Census U.S.A.: Fact Finding for the American People, 1790–1970.* New York: Seabury Press, 1968. (An exceptionally readable story of the census based upon much careful research.)

Temple University. *Survey of Federal Reorganization.* Philadelphia, 1953.

Texas. Legislative Council. *Laws Based on Population: A Report to the 58th Legislature.* Austin, 1962.

WILLCOX, WALTER F. *Studies in American Demography.* Ithaca: Cornell University Press, 1940.

ARTICLES AND PAPERS

BERSHAD, MAX A., and BENJAMIN J. TEPPING. "The Development of Household Sample Surveys." *Journal of the American Statistical Association,* December, 1969, pp. 1134–40.

BORDEN, NEIL H., et al. "An Appraisal of Census Programs for Marketing Uses." *The Journal of Marketing,* April, 1954, pp. 331–66.

Committee on Government Statistics and Information Services. *Government Statistics.* Social Science Research Council Bulletin 26. New York, 1937.

DALY, JOSEPH F. "Some Basic Principles of Statistical Surveys." *Journal of the American Statistical Association,* December, 1969, pp. 1129–33.

FALKNER, ROLAND P. *The Development of the Census.* A paper submitted to the American Academy of Political and Social Science, December 13, 1898 (No. 240).

FRANKEL, LESTER R. "Comments." *Journal of the American Statistical Association,* December, 1969, pp. 1152–53.

HANSEN, M. H., and W. N. HURWITZ. "On the Theory of Sampling from Finite Populations." *Annals of Mathematical Statistics,* December, 1943, pp. 333–62.

HANSEN, MORRIS H. "A Memorial for William N. Hurwitz." *Journal of the American Statistical Association,* December, 1969, pp. 1122–28.

HATHAWAY, WILLIAM A. "Internal and External Needs of American Business." *American Statistical Association Quarterly,* June, 1918, pp. 1–15.

NEYMAN, J. "On the Two Different Aspects of the Representative Method: The Method of Stratified Sampling and the Method of

Purposive Selection," *Journal of the Royal Statistical Society,* February, 1934, pp. 558–625.

ROSSITER, WILLIAM S. "The Present Status of Statistical Work and How it Needs to be Developed in the Service of the Federal Government." *ASA Quarterly,* June, 1914, pp. 85–96.

STEPHAN, FREDERICK F. "History of the Uses of Modern Sampling Procedures." *Journal of the American Statistical Association,* March, 1948, pp. 12–39.

Subcommittee on Criteria for Surveys for Other Federal Government Agencies. "Criteria for Undertaking Surveys for Other Federal Government Agencies." *American Statistician,* February, 1969, pp. 17–19.

WAKSBERG, JOSEPH, and LEON PRITZKER. "Changes in Census Methods." *Journal of the American Statistical Association,* December, 1969, pp. 1141–49.

WALKER, FRANCIS A. "The Eleventh Census of the United States." *Quarterly Journal of Economics,* January, 1888, pp. 135–61.

GOVERNMENT DOCUMENTS

DEBOW, J. D. B. *Statistical View of the United States: A Compendium of the Seventh Census.* Washington, 1854.

FISHBEIN, MEYER H. *The Censuses of Manufactures 1810–1890.* National Archives Accessions, No. 57. Washington, 1963.

HANNA, FRANK A. *The Compilation of Manufacturing Statistics.* Washington: Government Printing Office, 1959.

Intensive Review Committee to the Secretary of Commerce. *Appraisal of Census Programs.* Washington: Government Printing Office, 1954.

ROSSITER, W. L. *A Century of Population Growth.* Washington: Government Printing Office, 1909.

TRUESDELL, LEON E. *The Development of Punch Card Tabulation in the Bureau of the Census.* Washington: Government Printing Office, 1965.

U.S. Congress. Subcommittee on Economic Statistics of the Joint Economic Committee. *Review of Federal Statistical Programs.* Hearings April 30, May 1 and 15, 1969. 91st Congress, 1st Session. Washington: Government Printing Office, 1969.

U.S. Department of Commerce. Bureau of the Census. *The Story of the Census: 1790–1916.* Washington, 1917.

U.S. Department of Commerce and Labor. *Statistical Reorganization.* Washington, 1908.

U.S. Department of the Interior. *Annual Report of the Secretary of the Interior for 1861.* Washington, 1862.

U.S. Director of the Census. *The Census Office and Coordination of*

Statistics. (Reply to the inquiries of the Interdepartmental Statistical Committee). Washington, 1909.

U.S. House of Representatives. *Statistical Work of U.S. Government.* House Documents, vol. 96, 67th Congress, 2nd Session. Washington, 1922.

————. Subcommittee on Census and Statistics of the Committee on Post Office and Civil Service. *1970 Census and Legislation Related Thereto.* Hearings, April 1–June 17, 1969. Serial No. 91–8, Part I. 91st Congress, 1st Session. Washington: Government Printing Office, 1969.

————. ————. *1970 Census Plans.* Hearings, May 23, June 20–22, 1967. 90th Congress, 1st Session. Washington: Government Printing Office, 1967.

————. ————. *Report on Accuracy of the 1970 Census Enumeration.* 91st Congress, 2nd Session. Washington: Government Printing Office, 1970.

U.S. Senate. Committee on the Judiciary. *Hearings on S. 1564 to enforce the 15th Amendment to the Constitution of the United States.* 89th Congress, 1st Session. Washington: Government Printing Office, 1965.

————. Subcommittee of the Committee on Commerce. *1940 Censuses.* Hearings on S. Res. 231, 76th Congress, 3rd Session. Washington: Government Printing Office, 1940.

WRIGHT, CARROLL D., and WILLIAM C. HUNT. *The History and Growth of the United States Census.* Washington: Government Printing Office, 1900.

UNPUBLISHED

DURAND, E. DANA. *Memoirs of E. Dana Durand.* An unpublished autobiography copyrighted in 1954. (Copy available in Census Bureau Library.)

STOUFFER, S. A. *Problems of the Bureau of the Census in Their Relation to Social Science.* A Report to the Committee on Survey of Governmental Relations to Research, the National Resources Committee. Manuscript dated April 2, 1938. (Census Bureau Library.)

TAEUBER, CONRAD. *Developments in the Analysis and Use of Census Data: 1900–60.* Presented at Social Statistics Section Meeting of the American Statistical Association, April 21, 1961, Ithaca, New York.

Index

Index